MW00945585

To Tom & Linda

STEPPING OUT

OF THE PAGES

Bible Personalities Speak

Prov. 3:5 & 6

Karen K. Satterlee

KAREN K. SATTERLEE

Illustrations by Hoyle Wallace

Dedication

*T*his book is dedicated to the very special man of God I have shared my life with for over half a century! He has loved me unconditionally, and encouraged me every day in the writing of this book, as well as in so many aspects of my life and ministry! Phil R. Satterlee is my helpmate, my cheerleader, my dearest friend and confidant, and the best husband a woman could ask for! I love you, Honey!

Table of Contents

Old Testament Monologues

New Testament Monologues

Section I – Advent and Christmas

Section II – Stories Jesus Told

Section III – People Jesus Met

Section IV – Lent and Easter

Old and New Testament Monologues Combined

Section V – A Family Devotional Walk

Section VI – Sisters across the Centuries

Section VII – Special Topics

Introduction

*T*his book has been many years in the making, and is in fact a compilation of Biblical monologues written and performed over a span of 50+ years in the ministry.

The purpose of this book is to give insight and "life" to many different characters in the Bible – some named, some nameless, but all with a story to tell! Some of the storylines and characters are fictional, but the Scriptural truths have not been compromised or disregarded.

The monologues contained in this book are meant to be read in private or in a group setting, such as a Bible study.(A Study Guide has been provided at the back of the book to help stimulate discussion and deeper study into each character and story.) Also, these monologues may be performed in a public gathering. I personally have performed and/ or directed each monologue included in this compilation. I chose to perform them from memory, and with Biblical costuming to increase the effectiveness of each portrayal.

It is my sincere prayer and hope that you will find these character studies/ monologues to be enjoyable, but also to be a blessing and a challenge to your daily living as you think about the experiences and events related in these stories.

To God be all the glory for anything and everything that may be done for the extension of His Kingdom through this book!

A Servant of Christ,
Karen K. Satterlee

OLD TESTAMENT MONOLOGUE

Chapter 1

The Baby in a Basket

(Jochebed – as told by Miriam)

Texts: Genesis 41: 45, 50; Exodus 1: 1-2:10; 15: 1, 2(* Scripture quotes are from the NASB)

I can still see the determined, confident look on her moonlit face as she waded into the Nile River. She wanted to position that tiny hand-made ark with its precious cargo in just the right place. Under cover of darkness, she awaited the early morning arrival of the Princess she hoped would pity and protect her infant son.

Years of oppression had preceded that anxious night. At first, our people had prospered under the kind hand of the Pharaoh of Joseph's day. Indeed, our race was saved from starvation during the great famine in Israel. Given a portion of the land of Goshen, the family of Jacob found a welcome home in Egypt.

As time went on, the Hebrew population grew, and on the horizon appeared a new Pharaoh - who knew not Joseph, and the marvelous leadership he had given to all the peoples.

This Pharaoh perceived the Hebrews to be a threat - a strong people, multiplying like insects, and this Egyptian King thought the wealth of his country was in danger. Thus, he mounted a campaign of oppression, and we all became his slaves.

There was brutal treatment, hard back-breaking labor, unreasonable physical demands - with little or nothing in return. Still, our people thrived and our numbers increased.

When Pharaoh saw the unflagging strength and stamina of his Hebrew slaves, he became even more frustrated and frightened. Why, they could easily join forces with other enemies nearby, he thought, and overturn the Egyptian rule.

He worked us even harder in order to discourage and defeat us – but it didn't work! We kept up the pace, and our numbers kept growing! Then, consumed with jealousy and fear, the Pharaoh devised a plan to murder all Hebrew boy babies. The midwives were summoned to Pharaoh's court, and were actually TAUGHT how to murder the babies – much to their horror, and they were commanded by Pharaoh to carry out the plan!

Ah, but those courageous mid-wives feared God- and they did NOT do as the King of Egypt had commanded them - they let the boys live!

God protected those brave midwives for their obedience to Him - and Pharaoh came up with a new plan. He made a law for all of his people that all new born male Hebrew babies should be thrown into the Nile River! The people were empowered to carry this out.

Our humble servant home was situated in the Nile River Valley - near the city of On- and so it came to be that nearly every day, the anguished cries and screams of helpless mothers were heard up and down the valley, as angry Egyptians snatched up their baby boys and drowned them in the river!

I was so frightened when I learned that mother would soon give birth to another baby. Though I was just ten years of age, I was deeply affected by the Pharaoh's edict and knew in my heart the pain this could bring upon our family, should mother have a boy child.

I remember the night he was born - oh - he was beautiful! There was something very special, sacred and solemn about him - we all felt it imme- diately - this was a child of destiny! I was filled with awe and wonder - but I also wept to think that at any moment he could be seized from us and destroyed.

Mother had so much faith - she believed that God's mighty hand was upon my tiny brother - but she also had a plan for his protection. The first three months of his life, we kept him hidden - between the donkey stable and the grain storage room, we kept him secretly safe. Then, his cries began to grow louder and stronger - his presence was much more noticeable. I watched as the shadows of fear crossed mother's face. She knew she could no longer hide him.

One day, she took me with her down to the water's edge. I kept the baby hushed and watched as she carefully picked the tall papyrus reeds growing there. She spent several days weaving the reeds together, forming a basket. She lovingly lined the ark with tar, and then covered the outside entirely with pitch. She worked thoughtfully, prayerfully -silently. Then, at last, she shared her plan with me.

This was to be an ark of safety for my baby brother. We would place him in it - take him to the water's edge just before dawn, and wait and watch for the Pharaoh's daughter to come for her daily bath.

I saw my mother's faith lived out as she resolutely made her way to the River that misty night. She raised the lid of the basket one last time, and brushed his soft cheek with a kiss. Then stifling a sob, she ran back home.

I was positioned on the other side where I could see both the basket and the path the Princess always took to the shore. My heart pounded with anticipation, and I prayed that my dear mother would be comforted. It seemed like hours, though I am sure it was not - and at last I heard voices and the shuffling of feet along the path. Would mother's plan work? We were about to find out!

The Princess soon discovered the basket in the bulrushes - and calling to her maids, she requested it be brought to her. I held my breath as she lifted the cover. In a second she could simply overturn that little ark, and drown my brother - thus carrying out her father's orders. No one would stop her!

*But it seemed the light of love filled her face as she gazed upon the baby - "This is one of the Hebrew children", I heard her say. She could not take her eyes off him...I made my move from the bushes. "Shall I go and call a nurse for you from the Hebrew women – that she may nurse the child for you?" I asked. She smiled kindly and lovingly in my direction - "Go ahead!" she answered. She hardly had finished the words as I flew past the bushes and straight for my own little home on the other shore!

"Mother - mother!" I called as I reached the door..."She wants you....she saw the baby....she's going to save him, I know.....she wants you...she wants YOU to take care of him!"

With excitement and feet winged with joy, we ran back to the Princess. Holding the baby now in her arms, the daughter of Pharaoh passed him ever so gently to my mother......to HIS mother.... 'Take this child away and nurse him for me, and I will give you your wages" she said. I could hardly believe my ears...not only would mother be able to care for my brother, but the Princess would PAY her for it! Truly God had answered our prayers.... more than we could have imagined- in ways far beyond our understanding.

Thus, mother was able to care for my brother the first several years of his life - instilling in him a deep belief and trust in God. She imparted to him the sacred traditions of the Hebrew people, and the divine promise given to Abraham and his descendants that God would make of them a great nation. Imagine! She it was who rocked him to sleep each night, and watched him romp and play each day inside the Pharaoh's Palace. Incredible, unbelievable events that God alone had orchestrated, but mother had trusted him with all her heart!

Mother did not live to see Moses become the great leader and emancipator of our people. Truly, this "Prince of Egypt" became one of the greatest men to ever set foot on this earth.....and Aaron - became the first High priest and spokesman for Moses.

And even I, Miriam, became one of the first women leaders for our people -a "prophetess" - inspired to teach the will of God. God gave me the courage to lead the people in song as we passed through the Red Sea on dry ground....with tambourine in hand, I danced and sang....."I will sing to the Lord, for He is highly exalted. The horse and its rider he has hurled into the sea.....the Lord is my strength and my song; He has become my salvation!"

It is no accident that there came forth THREE great leaders from one family....it happened because my mother, Jochebed, was obedient and faithful. In the face of danger, she trusted God, and worked alongside Him to fulfill His plan for her life, and ours.

All my days, I will praise the Lord for the blessing of a godly mother, who showed us by her life how to trust the Living God!

NEW TESTAMENT MONOLOGUES
SECTION I- ADVENT AND CHRISTMAS

The following FOUR monologues.....

Mary's Joy (The Annunciation)

Mary's Journey (To Elizabeth)

Mary's Judgment (her claim to be a virgin with child)

Mary's Jesus (The birth)

were used in our morning worship services – one each Sunday during Advent.

"Mary" appeared each Sunday, somewhere during the service, and then our pastor picked up the theme in his morning messages.

Obviously, they can be used in various ways, and as stand-alone monologues.

However, I thought it would be helpful to know how they were originally presented.

Chapter 2:

Mary's Joy

(The Annunciation)

Text: Luke 1: 1-38
(All quotes are from MSG)

*C*hildren – children – come along – come sit with me here by the manger!

Can you imagine what it was like to be visited by a real angel – right in your own home?

Well, that is what happened to me and I tell you I was terrified! Have you ever been really, really afraid?

There I was, sitting at the weaving loom, as I did most every day – except that day, I was day dreaming – thinking about my beloved Joseph and our coming wedding. In fact, I was making wedding plans in my head when suddenly there was a light and an unmistakable presence right there with me – and I knew it was a messenger from God!

"Good morning!" he said. "You are beautiful with God's beauty – beautiful inside and out and God is with you!"

I was shaking with fright, wondering what such a greeting meant!

"Mary," the angel continued, "You have nothing to fear! God has a surprise for you! You will become pregnant and give birth to a son and call his name Jesus. He will be great, and be called the Son of the Highest. The Lord will give him the throne of his father David; He will rule Jacob's house forever – no end, ever to his kingdom."

Gabriel was the angel's name – and he was talking about the Messiah – the Promised One of God for whom we had all been waiting for so very long! I knew that sooner or later someone would be chosen as the one to bring the Messiah into the world – and that someone would be the most blessed among women. But never, never in my wildest dreams could I have imagined that someone would be me!

Yet, there stood Gabriel right in front of me – telling me that God had chosen ME! Me – a humble peasant girl – barely a teenager – God had chosen me!

My fear gave way to incredible joy! Messiah was coming, and I was part of the plan!

Of course I had questions, but Gabriel simply said, "Nothing , you see, is impossible with God. The Holy Spirit will come upon you and the power of the Highest hover over you. Therefore the child you bring to birth will be called Holy, Son of God!"

Our darkness would soon be over – the Light was coming! Our prayers would soon be answered – Jesus was coming!

"Yes – YES!" I said to Gabriel. "I am the Lord's maid – ready to serve. Let it be with me just as you say!"

The angel left as quickly as he had come – but joy filled my whole being as I danced around our little Nazareth home. Jesus was coming – the greatest Christmas present of all – and I had been chosen to deliver the gift!

Children, the greatest joy in all the world is found in doing God's will! Whatever it is that He asks you to do – say "Yes, Lord, YES! I'm here – and I'm ready!"

Chapter 3:

Mary's Journey

(To Elizabeth)

Texts: Luke 1: 39-56
(All Scripture quotes are from MSG)

*I*t was a long rough trip to Hebron – nearly a four day journey by caravan. But, it gave me plenty of time to think – to ponder – to re-live the dramatic visitation of God's messenger, Gabriel, to our little Nazareth home – and to me, in particular.

I needed to get away – away from the curious looks – the wagging tongues – the whispered doubts. I needed to "clear my head" mother had said – to make certain in my heart and mind that my encounter with Gabriel had been real, and not just a vivid daydream at the weaving loom.

Gabriel had told me that my cousin Elizabeth was with child – six months along already. Mother and I agreed that my going to visit Elizabeth might well do us both good. I think Mother needed time, too – to seek God's confirmation in her own heart that my story – my amazing announcement of God's purpose for my life was really true.

Elizabeth was no young woman. She and Zechariah were well up in years- she well past child bearing age. For years she had suffered the scorn and shame of being childless – "the barren one" they called her in their cynical circles of gossip. She had endured much pain through all those years.

I tried to picture what she would look like – white-haired Elizabeth, great with child! It was a picture that made me smile – actually, it made me laugh out loud as I remembered Gabriel's words – "Nothing, you see, is impossible with God!"

Surely we were kindred spirits – her with her impossible pregnancy, and me with mine. I was bursting to talk with her about it all – I had been keeping it all inside – and I could not wait to be with her!

Elizabeth was not expecting me. How her face lit up with joy when she saw me – and then, she spoke. "You're so blessed among women and the babe in your womb, also blessed! And why am I so blessed that the mother of my Lord visits me?" She told me that as soon as she heard my voice – the babe in her womb "skipped like a lamb for sheer joy!"

I was so touched, comforted and relieved by her words that I collapsed into her arms! God used Elizabeth's greeting as a most wonderful balm to me – affirmation – what a precious gift! Oh, how Elizabeth's words flooded my soul with bright hope and encouragement. Suddenly I felt a sense of purpose and worth once more.

I could not help but praise God! All along that long journey I had been reciting the psalms of praise and promises from the Scriptures – trying to absorb the awesome part God had chosen me to play in history. I could contain the song no longer – Praise Him! Praise Him!

There, at the beginning of an awesome journey – one I alone was chosen to travel, my eyes, my thoughts, my heart had to be on God! I realized and expressed in my song that God's resources are endless – that nothing is impossible with Him – and that His love makes any hardship able to be carried with joy!

Chapter 4:

Mary's Judgment

(Her claim to be a virgin with child)

Text: Matthew 1: 18-25
Scripture quotes are from NKJV)

They were all there waiting for me when I returned home from Hebron – the cynics – the critics – the gossips. Word had spread quickly in the small town of Nazareth and since I had been gone for 3 months, there was plenty of time for the stories against me to heat up and to be spewed out in venomous sentences of judgment and whispered accusations, spreading like wildfire!

Everywhere I went I heard it – in the market place – at the well – even people simply passing by our home would wag their heads in pretended sorrow for such a "harlot" as me!

"My soul magnifies the Lord, and my spirit has rejoiced in God my Savior" – I kept reminding myself over and over. But the worst hurt of all came within the confines of my own household. Mother seemed more accepting of the truth – it was obvious to me that she had sought and found God's peace regarding the matter while I was with Elizabeth and Zechariah.

But father – father would barely look at me, let alone speak to me. When I did catch his eye, I saw such sorrow, hurt and disappointment. He had poured so much of himself into my life – and now I had failed him – or so he thought. He was embarrassed and humiliated and how was I to fix that?

"My soul magnifies the Lord"..."Do not be afraid, Mary, for you have found favor with God ..." How I clung to Elizabeth's affirmation of my being the "mother of her Lord"! God alone would have to carry me through this pain.

And then there was my beloved Joseph. He had already heard the rumors – now he needed to hear it from me. He came that first evening after I returned. As we walked together in the moonlight, I told him everything – every word as I remembered it – from Gabriel's greeting to Elizabeth's gracious affirmation.

How could I expect Joseph to believe me? It was an impossible tale. I saw his heart break right before my eyes. First, the red of anger rushed to his face – and then just as quickly all the color drained from him and I thought he might faint. He stumbled away from me into the night – weeping – no, sobbing under the weight of such a racking revelation.

What could I do? What could I say? I knew God had chosen Joseph, too! He knew what a wonderful stepfather he would be for God's Son. But it was out of my hands. Somehow, God would need to speak directly to Joseph, as He had to me through Gabriel.

I returned home. There was no sleep for me that night – just tears – tears and prayers and prayers and tears – trusting God alone to bring the healing for all the hurt!

Even before daylight I heard them – voices raised in anger from the street below my window. I recognized them – town officials – religious leaders – faces contorted in judgment – rocks clutched in their hands – shouting – SHOUTING... .."Liar" – "Adulterer" – "Blasphemer."

"Stone her! Stone her! Justice must be done! Drag her into the street and publically stone her to death!"

This would NOT be my fate! God would not allow this! I was bearing His Son – He would not die before He was born! "God – God", I cried, "Please make a way for me!"

Suddenly there was a hurried knock at the front door. Father went to answer it, certain it was some of the people who were shouting – but it was my Joseph, asking for me! I ran down the steps into his arms! His face was shining with glory! In a flood of emotion, he told me his experience. An angel of the Lord had appeared to him in a dream telling him to marry me – that I was telling the truth and God had indeed chosen me to bear His Son.

"There will be a wedding after all" he said, twirling me around off my feet. "To think I have been chosen, too – to help you care for God's Son!"

In a moment the pain had become praise! Father had heard all that Joseph had said and he came to my side to embrace the two of us in his arms!

Two obscure lives, from an obscure village called Nazareth would now be thrust upon the world stage with an influence and experience that would change everything for eternity! How humbling – how incredibly exciting that God was allowing us to live it together! Together we would face our future as husband and wife. Together Joseph and I would raise God's Son who would change the course of history forever with His redeeming love! Together, with God's help and strength, we would overcome the negative darts being hurled at us – knowing that we are part of an amazing miracle!

Chapter 5:

Mary's Jesus

(The Birth)

Texts: Luke 2: 1-35

*A*ll of our earthly possessions we could bring along were piled high on Old Beaut, Joseph's aging donkey. Nazareth was behind us – would we ever return? Mother and father had wept so at our leaving – nearly broke my heart to see them so pained.

But, we had no choice. Caesar Augustus had mandated a census and taxation – requiring each person to return to the city of their ancestry. Since Joseph and I were both from the line of King David, that meant we had to journey to Bethlehem, just a few miles outside of Jerusalem.

It was nearly time for the birth – what a time to travel – and on foot at that. At times I felt I could go no further – my swollen feet longed for some cool stream or a healing balm of oil – my back throbbed with pain of the extra weight I carried – the child within kicked to get out!

It was all part of God's plan, though – I knew it! I had already experienced so much of His goodness and grace to me – I knew that He knew exactly where I was along this dusty, rocky road – and He would not leave me comfortless!

Bethlehem had such a great history – being the home of King David – of Naomi, Ruth and Boaz – and the burial place for Jacob's beloved Rachel – but it was a small town – little but a rest stop on the access road to Jerusalem. Still, as I had much time to think about it – I recalled the prophet Micah had said that out of Bethlehem would come a" ruler over Israel, one whose origins are from of old – from ancient times." Surely it was that ruler I was carrying – and it was no accident we were on the road to Bethlehem!

We spent a night with Elizabeth and Zechariah on our journey – how good to sleep in the comfort of their home and not have to use Joseph's saddle bag for my pillow. But more importantly, seeing Elizabeth again gave me that last thrust of encouragement I needed to finish the journey. "Her Lord" as she kept calling Him, would be delivered soon – at the next full moon she said. We had to hasten on and not linger.

It was a party atmosphere when we arrived in Bethlehem - crowds of people – raucous music

– loud laughter and street vendors shouting their sales pitches. I was so tired – I just wanted to lie down in some quiet corner – anywhere – it really didn't matter. Joseph did his best to find accommodations for us at the local Inn – pleading for shelter and safety for the birthing.

Seems there was not a room to be had, though I think if we had not been such poor peasants many rooms might have become available.

At last we were led by the lantern of the Innkeeper to the stable-cave some distance from the Inn. Joseph wanted to keep trying to find a better place – but I knew – this WAS the place – the right place – some fresh straw and a blanket was all I really needed. The Innkeeper's wife brought what we needed, including some water, and she told us we could keep the lantern. So we settled in.

Just a few hours after we arrived, my son was born. We wrapped Him in strips of cloth we had brought from home and laid Him in a manger – the only cradle available in our stark surroundings. The cattle, sheep and oxen hushed as if they sensed the presence of the Divine – and Joseph held Him proudly and declared to all our furry friends – "His name is Jesus – because He will save His people from their sins!"

God said we should call Him Jesus – Savior. It was a mission statement for His life. It was His name – it was His reason from coming down to mankind. There was a message in the NAME, and

God did not want anyone to miss it! The world may be against us – beat us down – belittle us – but He is FOR us! He came to lift us up! GOD SAVES! – JESUS SAVES!

In the middle of the night the visitors came to see the newborn King. They were not the merchants or the monarchs – prophets or priests - not the soldiers or scholars – no; they were the lowly shepherds, come fresh from the Judean hillsides where they were "keeping watch over their flocks at night." Their faces glowed with glory as they spoke of an angel who told them a Savior had been born and where they could find Him – and of thousands of angels singing "Glory – glory to God in the highest heaven!" They all talked at once, and they could not stop talking – until they saw Him – Jesus!

Then, in a hallowed hush they knelt as one before this stranger in the straw. There was no doubt – this was the One the angels had spoken about – this was the One about whom they had sung His Glory song! Such absolute amazement filled their rugged faces with radiance, as tears of wonder and joy splashed upon the stable floor!

Why would God send such a magnificent word to such a lowly bunch? Because it is the meek souls who will receive Him – the humble and simple who see their own need and take time to come to Him, who came for them!

The shepherds told everyone they met about Jesus, but no one else came that night. Surely others had seen the heavenly fireworks and heard the incredible angel choir – but only the shepherds came – they came to the Lamb of God – to the one who would call Himself the Good Shepherd – and who would in the end, lay down His life for His sheep! They came – everyone else missed it – that night of wonder – that Holy Night!

How I pondered this all in my heart. In those moments of reflection, God also did something else for me – He showed me glimpses of Jesus' life – pulled back the curtain of things to come – a revelation of the reasons Jesus came. This rejection in Bethlehem was just the beginning. He would one day be "despised and rejected by mankind, a man of suffering, and familiar with pain." He would take upon Himself the sins of the whole world, and He would suffer and die for those sins in order to become our Savior. He who came down to us – would be lifted up – to draw all men unto Himself!

Simeon was right when he said,"… a sword will pierce your own soul too." How hard it was watching Him grow up and seeing the hatred mounting against Him – watching Him die in agony the cruel cross death of a common criminal.

Ah, but He came to be MY Savior, too! Still, in my humanness through every stage and experience of His life – I was His mother – it was a fact that could never be changed – and He – He was still my little child!

Chapter 6:

The Innkeeper's Wife

Texts: Luke 2: 1 – 40 (NLT); Matthew 2: 1-23; Luke 23: 26 -43

*I*t was a maddening night here in Bethlehem, I can tell you! Our quiet little town – normally a mere rest stop on the way to Jerusalem – was suddenly bursting with travelers and visitors from all over Israel.

This is the "city of David", and by decree of Caesar Augustus himself, anyone who was a descendant of King David had to travel to this town for a roll call and census. This was really a way for Rome to line its pockets! Caesar was looking for a head count that would translate into every shekel he could squeeze from the people of his kingdom.

And so, the little town was overrun with aunts and uncles and cousins of the third and fourth generations! Imagine those crowded streets! The census was a ripe time for innkeepers and vendors of every sort, but also for sticky-fingered thieves who could simply melt into the crowds. Taverns and Inns were bursting at the seams, and women of questionable character lingered in the shadows. People from every age and stage of life were there – the young, the old, the rich, the poor, the good, the bad, and all the ones in between! There was just no way that tiny Bethlehem could accommodate all those travelers with a comfortable night's rest! Some folks were bound to be turned away – it couldn't be helped!

I was bone weary, tending to all the travelers Rueben and I had taken in. Every room, every conceivable nook and cranny of our Wayside Inn was filled to overflowing. There were people – and animals everywhere! And what a noisy lot! They were ready to party, and I was ready to drop into the refuge of my own bed – when yet another knock sounded at our door. "Let Rueben get that one," I thought, "he is better at turning folks away, even though I know there is honestly no more room."

Still, I couldn't help being curious. I heard muffled conversation – and then it seemed to become desperate pleading on the part of the travelers. The accent was definitely Galilean – they had come a great distance, for sure. Something drew me to the window to have a look. There were two of them – a tall bearded man, and a very young, ashen-faced woman. She looked sad, and so very weary. Rueben shut the door and the couple turned to leave. It was then I saw them silhouetted in the moonlight. Why, the young girl was heavy with child – no wonder she was tired and worn! No wonder there was desperation in the husband's voice. Forgetting my own weariness, I bounded through the back door of the Inn and out into the crowded streets. I must find them - and soon! I was sure that baby could come at any moment.

I caught up with them as they were going around the corner to the next street.

"Wait, wait!" I called out to them. They stopped and turned toward me. I was out of breath from running!

"I am Leah – my husband Rueben and I own the Inn you just left. It is true, we haven't an inch of room left, but I know you need a place to rest. There is a large stable behind our Inn. Unfortunately, there are many more animals there tonight than usual – but still it is clean and warm and quiet. I can make a bed for you there!"

"I am Joseph," the man said, "and this is my wife, Mary. We would be grateful for any place to lay our heads – my wife is with child and...."

"I know, I know," I interrupted, "and there is no time to lose! You go around back and I will meet you there with some blankets and fresh straw."

My feet felt winged, and my heart felt lighter than it had in years! I hummed as I gathered things for their comfort. Rueben did not know what had come over me – and there was no time to explain. I filled a large basin with water, and gathered some towels, too.

They were already in the stable when I arrived. At least some of the strain was gone from their faces – they were away from all that pushing and shoving and drinking and cursing. But as I was arranging the blankets and straw, I heard Mary begin to moan, and I suspected the pains of labor had begun.

"I am a midwife," I told them. "I have helped deliver many babies here in Bethlehem. If you want, I will stay with you and help Mary deliver your child. You will owe me nothing."

The relief was evident in their faces – "Please – yes – thank you!" they kept repeating. For some strange reason, I felt as though I should be thanking them!

Just then Caleb, our hired hand, came to check on the animals. He was startled to find people in the stable! "It is all right, Caleb" I said, "the animals all seem hushed and settled for the night. But please give Rueben a message for me – tell him I am assisting in the birth of a baby – right here in our stable!"

"Yes, Ma'am" Caleb nodded as he backed nervously out the door. "I surely will tell him, Ma'am."

"Good," I thought, "now Rueben will not worry about me on this most unusual Bethlehem night!"

Joseph paced back and forth when he wasn't comforting Mary. He also appeared to be praying. For a young mother-to-be, Mary seemed calm and determined. In the midst of her pain, she was radiant! In fact, I had never before witnessed such strength in such a young girl. She cooperated with me throughout the whole birthing process, and within a few short hours, she brought forth a healthy baby boy! Now Joseph was radiant!

We shall "...give him the name Jesus," he said, "because He will save His people from their sins."

Not an unusual name. There were many named Jesus during that time. It was a common name for boys, being the Greek equivalent of "Joshua" which means "God saves" – and calling to mind the great leader of Israel who succeeded Moses. No, the name was not unusual, but it was the other part of Joseph's proclamation that stayed with me – "He shall save His people from their sins."

Israel needed to be saved. Many of our people were confused, doubtful, cynical, faithless and bitter. Lost, in a word. The glory days were behind us, and the Messianic prophesies seemed like a long forgotten dream.

What were some of those prophesies? He would be born of a virgin.....He will be the greatest of all, and He will end our struggle and free us forever....the prophet Micah had even declared that He would be born in Bethlehem!

I was lost in this reverie – until suddenly I became aware of much commotion and confusion around me. Strangers had invaded the stable – a large number of them. The scent of sheep was everywhere and I recognized the visitors. The despised sheepherders from the fields had come to town. Why here? Why now? In the middle of the night!

I protested – "You can't just come in here unannounced like this – there is a new born baby here!" I stopped short of remarking about all the smell and filth they brought with them. They never heard a word I said. They were transfixed – mesmerized by the infant. They knelt in the straw, talking amongst themselves about "angels –anthems – and announcement of great news"! They pointed to the baby, whom we had lovingly placed in a manger. "It is just as the angel told us," one shepherd said, "wrapped in cloths and lying in a manger!" They began to shout praises to God, as tears streamed down their ruddy faces.

Mary and Joseph seemed to take it all in stride – not surprised by the uninvited guests – not at all hesitant to share their treasured infant with these lowly sheepherders. I stood amazed! How could those shepherds have known to come to our stable? Why would they make such a trip for his baby? A holy hush fell on that smelly cattle stall and made it into a cathedral!

For a long time after they left, we could hear those shepherds shouting and praising God – and telling everyone they met about the baby in a manger!

Morning was coming. The first light of dawn began to creep across the floor of the stable. Mary slept, Joseph nodded – the baby cooed sweetly in His slumber. I wasn't needed anymore – but I didn't want to leave. Something in my heart told me I had been part of a miracle – a miracle that was just beginning. It was truly a night of wonder!

For several days, Mary, Joseph and the baby remained in the stable. I carried them meals, and made sure baby Jesus had everything He needed. I listened intently to Mary and Joseph as they shared the intimate details of their encounters with angels. Mary declared she was a virgin, and that Jesus was God's Son, born of her because the Holy Spirit had overshadowed her. She told me of the rejection she had experienced in Nazareth – how some of the religious leaders were ready to stone her to death because of her pregnancy. Even Joseph understandably had his doubts – feeling betrayed and ready to divorce Mary until an angel had told him in a dream that Mary was speaking the truth, and he should proceed with their plans to marry.

My head was spinning with all these stories which seemed so astonishing. Yet, I could not deny that this Jesus was having a profound effect upon my life.

Mary and Joseph made the journey to the temple in Jerusalem when Jesus was just a few days old. This was to offer a sacrifice and dedicate the child to God. When they returned, Mary was glowing!

"An elderly, godly man named Simeon recognized Jesus," she said. "He came to us with tears streaming down his wrinkled face. At first we were startled, then we realized the presence of the Holy Spirit, and we gladly allowed Simeon to hold Jesus. He began to speak with undeniable strength and authority."

"Sovereign Lord, as you have promised, you may now dismiss your servant in peace. For my eyes have seen your salvation, which you have prepared in the sight of all nations: a light for revelation to the Gentiles, and the glory of your people Israel."

Joseph told me a prophetess named Anna was also at the Temple – and when she saw Jesus, she declared to everyone that He was the promised Messiah!

It was exciting, but at the same time confusing for me. Wouldn't Messiah come in a majestic, powerful way? In a way that everyone would recognize Him and worship Him? Wouldn't He ride into town in triumph - overturning rulers and governments and establishing His kingdom? Surely

He wouldn't come as a tiny, helpless baby! Still, I wondered.

Rueben and I helped Mary and Joseph move into a home in Bethlehem, and for many months, it seemed like they had settled into a very normal life. I visited them often. Jesus was learning to walk and talk, and delighting Mary and Joseph with His toddler antics.

Then, another very unusual thing happened. One night a large caravan of camels and men from the East arrived in Bethlehem. They looked like kings, handsome and finely dressed. Their parade went right past our Inn. They seemed to be on a mission. It was whispered in the streets that they had been in Jerusalem, inquiring of King Herod where "the King of the Jews" had been born. They were following His star, so they said, and it led them to Bethlehem! We watched from our doorway as they disappeared down the street and then stopped – at the home of Joseph and Mary! There was a brilliant star lighting up the whole sky – and it did seem to be positioned over their little home! Three of the strangers dismounted and entered the home. The town was abuzz about this curious invasion. People were gathered in doorways and hanging out of windows trying to get a glimpse of these majestic travelers. After a while, the 3 emerged from the house, mounted their camels, and left town by a different road than they had come. I couldn't wait to talk to Mary about this! I ran down the street!

They were still in awe when I arrived. Jesus was seated on Mary's lap, and at her feet were 3 gifts the visitors had brought for Jesus, Mary said. There was Frankincense, gold, and myrrh. Strange gifts to give a toddler – expensive, rare gifts! I learned that those travelers were astrologers and recognized that brilliant star as a sign that a king had been born – and not just ANY king – OUR king – King of the Jews! They had been following that star for months and it had led them to Bethlehem, and right to the exact place where Jesus was! Quite a contrast to those simple shepherds who visited Jesus in the stable, these were educated and influential men. They had come a great distance to worship Him too. What did it all mean? As I said goodnight, and walked back to the Inn, I was once again filled with wonder!

We were awakened the next morning by shouting in the streets. Then we heard the heartbreaking sobs of some of the village women. What was happening now? A messenger knocked on our door with the news. Herod was irate because of the visitors from the east. The idea that there could possibly be another King infuriated him – so much so, that he "...gave orders to kill all the boys in Bethlehem and its vicinity who were two years old and under, in accordance with the time he had learned from the Magi." No wonder there was such weeping and wailing in the streets! How thankful I was that our sons were well beyond that age. Then, the horror of that decree struck me. The young child Jesus was in grave danger! Dressing quickly, I ran down the street to the home of Mary and Joseph. There was no answer at the door. Was I too late to warn them? Had the hideous crime already been carried out?

Finally the next door neighbor opened her door. "They have gone," Deborah said, "got up and left in the middle of the night. They said they were fleeing to Egypt to protect their young son – something about a dream and an angel. That's all I can tell you."

I thanked her, and walked slowly back home. I was thankful they were safe, but I was also overcome with a sinking feeling that I would never again see that special young child or his parents. I wept for the emptiness I felt in my soul.

Years passed – life changed – and as I feared, I did not see Mary, Joseph or Jesus again. Rueben died, my oldest son was helping me at the Inn, but my youngest son had broken my heart with his wicked ways. He became so wayward that he was sentenced to die for his crimes of thievery. Heavy hearted, I one day found myself on the outskirts of Jerusalem, climbing a rugged hill overlooking the city dump. I was there to witness my son's execution by way of crucifixion. This was a common occurrence in Jerusalem, but there seemed to be a great amount of anger and hatred being expressed toward one of the criminals in particular – it was the one on the middle cross. He was badly beaten – His face torn and swollen – and He was wearing a crown made from thorns. My own grief and pain seemed to pale in comparison as I considered what the mother of that man must be going through. I approached her as she sobbed at the foot of his cross. I knelt beside her, and as she turned to face me, I could not believe my eyes – it was Mary!

We fell together in a heap, weeping for our sons, but weeping for the joy of seeing one another! I realized in an instant that man on the middle cross was Jesus – the tiny baby I had helped to deliver so long ago!

"Why, Mary?" I managed to ask, amidst my sobs.

"It's all a part of God's plan, Leah. Remember, He came to be our Savior – we all need Him, and He is dying now for your sins and mine! From the stable to this cross, it's all been God's plan, and today, Leah, Jesus is finishing the work God sent Him to do!"

Just then, Jesus spoke from the cross – "Father, forgive them, for they do not know what they are doing."

The other thief beside Jesus shouted to Him – "Aren't you the Messiah? Save yourself and us!"

Then I heard my son's voice. "Don't you fear God," he said, "since you are under the same sentence? We are punished justly, for we are getting what our deeds deserve. But this man has done nothing wrong."

Then he turned to speak to Jesus. "Jesus, remember me when you come into your kingdom."

Jesus looked at my son with such love in His eyes – "Truly I tell you, today you will be with me in paradise."

In a moment, I saw the whole picture. The little baby we had crowded out of our Inn had made room for my sinner son – for every sinner. I opened my heart to Him that day – amidst the darkness, the earthquakes – the thunder and storms all around. I experienced the presence of Jesus born in my heart! His peace filled my soul like nothing I had ever experienced before. I gave Him the room that was most important – my heart!

He is the Messiah – He is the Savior! You see, the birth of Jesus brought God to mankind, but the cross of Jesus brings mankind to God!

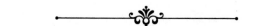

SECTION II- STORIES JESUS TOLD

Chapter 7:

Don't Miss the Party!

(Mother of the Prodigal)

Text: Luke 15:11-32
(* Scripture quotes are from NLT,
**** Quotes are from MSG)**

*G*et out the linen tablecloths and napkins! Polish the silver vessels and golden trays! There is going to be a party! We have reason to rejoice. Our hearts are overflowing with joy and thanksgiving!

Oh, but it has been a long time coming. For many months our hearts have been heavy and burdened with sorrows only a parent could know. With pain no words can describe.

It began when our youngest son, Seth became restless with his life at home. The sights and sounds of the city began to call him away from our simple life in the valley. At first, he would go away for a night or two – he had friends in town, he said. We worried, but he always came back. Then one day, he boldly asked his father for his share of the inheritance – money that should rightfully be his only after his father's death. He wanted to get out on his own – to leave home – for good!

Joseph, my husband, was grieved by Seth's request. He was so young – so innocent – so untouched by the world. To give in to him would surely send him further into his pursuit of the world – a world we were not sure he was prepared to resist! On the other hand, to refuse him would only add fuel to the fire of rebellion rising in his restless heart. Long into the night Joseph and I talked and prayed, and wept together.

When the light of morning came, we had settled in our minds that we would grant his request. He clutched the money greedily, muttered his polite thanks, and brushed my cheek with a hurried kiss. His horse was laden with changes of garments, some of his favorite foods, and skins of water. Silently, painfully, we watched him ride off through the garden toward the mountains. How long would he be gone? Who would look after him? What kind of friends would he become associated with? Would he ever think about home again – about Joseph and me?

Early the next morning, Joseph arose and quickly stepped out onto the porch. Shielding his eyes from the rising sun, he scanned the horizon

– back and forth, back and forth, back and forth.
East to west – as far as his eyes could see! He
returned to that place again at midday – with the
sun high overhead. Again, he raised his eyes to the
horizon, watching intently each movement and
shadow. At evening, too, as the sun was setting
behind our little house, he looked longingly down
the road toward the mountains.

Thus it became his ritual – every day – faithfully, to watch for that familiar figure coming in
the distance – his son – coming home!

How it made my heart ache to see his eyes fill
with tears, to hear the heavy sighs as he turned
from his lookout place. Sometimes we would sit
silently at supper – another sunset gone, and no
Seth returned!

As we looked deep into each other's eyes, we
could see the pain of the other, and reaching a
hand across the table, we understood. Each new
day dawned with the hope that THIS could be the
day – and each evening, a grey curtain of disappointment fell when we knew it was not! Only
God knew where he was, and only God could
comfort us. All we could do was pray – and hope
– and wait!

In the meantime, as we were to later learn, Seth
was squandering the inheritance his father had
given him. He befriended people who delighted
in helping him spend his fortune – fancy clothes
– eating – drinking – harlots. It was a time of

rampant sin and debauchery. So far – so far from home! And – when the money was gone, so were his friends.

At the same time his goods ran out, there arose a great famine in that country and he began to be in want. He became so desperate, that he was willing to hire himself out as a servant – and not a respectable servant at that. In fact, he found himself feeding a herd of swine! Dirty, greedy, noisy swine! Imagine this fine Jewish boy up to his knees in the mire of a pig pen! Aye Yi yi! What a contrast from the gorgeous gardens of home!

Seth told us later that he was so hungry; he was ready to eat the carob pods he was feeding to the swine! He said at that lowest point of his life, he came to himself – to his senses. I think rather, he came to the end of himself – and found the beginning of God!

*"At home, even the hired servants have food enough to spare, and here I am dying of hunger!" What might they be having tonight? Stew – Venison – Roast lamb? His mouth watered, and his stomach writhed with hunger pangs. He purposed in his heart to return to his home.

*"I will go home to my father", he thought. He even rehearsed his speech of repentance over and over again.

*"Father, I have sinned against both heaven and you, and I am no longer worthy of being called your son. Please take me on as a hired servant."

The more he said it, the more determined he was to do it. "I will go home to my father." And he did!

Oh, I shall never forget that day – my Joseph was standing on the porch, looking over toward those mountains as he did every day – squinting – straining to see some movement, some stirring. When suddenly, he called to me – "Priscilla, it's him! He's coming a great way off – it's our Seth – he's coming home!"

By the time I reached the porch, Joseph was halfway across the field, leaping like an antelope! Seth was trudging slowly, as if under a great burden – but when he saw his father running toward him, he began to run, too! I watched with indescribable joy as they fell into each other's arms, and with mingled tears and laughter embraced one another.

*Remembering his rehearsed speech, Seth began to spill it out of his contrite heart. "Father, I have sinned against both heaven, and you, and I am no longer worthy of being called your son..."

**Joseph would not even let him finish. Calling to our servants he said, "Quick. Bring a clean set of clothes and dress him. Put the family ring on his finger and sandals on his feet. Then get a grain-fed heifer and roast it. We're going to feast! We're going to have a wonderful time! My son is here – given up for dead and now alive! Given up for lost and now found!"

Ah, it was a beautiful sight – that return – that reunion! Seth stumbled home humbly willing to become a hired hand – uncertain of how he would be received, perhaps even fearing rejection! Oh, but his father's love was unconditional – embracing – forgiving – restoring – clothing him in the garments of grace!

He came home filthy – and was cleansed! He returned in rags – and his father called for the finest robe! He ashamedly trudged home in disgrace – and was extended his father's grace, mercy and forgiveness! He came home worn, empty and hungry – and we are enjoying a bounteous feast in his honor!

Ah, my broken "mother heart" was healed in an instant – to see him coming home! God is faithful! As much as we love our Seth, God loves him so much more. He was ever with us—but He was also with our son, as we trusted Him to be! Thank you God, for helping us to never lose hope!

Come along now – you can come too! Oh, yes! The party is for everyone, you know. Why, even the angels in heaven rejoice over one sinner who repents – one child who comes home! It's amazing – this love of our Heavenly Father! Don't miss the party!

Benjamin – come along now – where are you? It's your brother – he's come home! There is great cause for rejoicing!

Oh Benjamin, Benjamin – don't miss the party!

Chapter 8:

Room at the Table

(The Parable of the Great Banquet)

Text: Luke 14: 15 – 24; Isaiah 55:1
(* Scripture Quotes are from The Voice)

*I*t was quite a feast. Quite a spectacle to behold! In fact, I would not believe it if I had not been there and seen it for myself.

My Master, (he's such a good man –so kind and gracious) he's always giving parties and having guests for dinner. It's just an ongoing thing for him (and I should be glad – otherwise, I would probably not be one of his hired servants!)Usually, he invites people very formally – written invitations. Then it's door to door chariot service – flowers – music –dancing—wine and tables sagging with every kind of food imaginable! He knows how to give a party!

But a few days ago, he sent out many gold-plated invitations, and then yesterday when the servant went to the home of those invited to announce that all things were now ready – no one came! Can you believe it? Not one of the invited guests showed up! We had outdone ourselves, too – the best china, the finest linens – a sumptuous banquet of fish, melons, almonds, figs, grapes, breads and pure olive oil I pressed myself! It was a feast fit for a king! There were hired musicians – we had the harp, the flute and the dulcimer. And then there were the golden lamps and chandeliers – the silver bowls and chalices – it was absolutely extravagant – the finest the Master could offer!

Ah, and you should have heard the excuses those people gave for not coming.

One had just bought a piece of land and needed to go and take a look at it – as if that land was just going to get up and walk away if he didn't go and see it right at that moment. Another had just purchased some oxen, and he wanted to go and try them out – as if they would have been too old and feeble to work that field for him the next day! Still another man had recently taken a wife and wanted to spend time with her. Why, he could have brought her – and the whole wedding party for that matter – there was plenty of room, and plenty of food!

But none of them came. Excuses, excuses! I cannot imagine rejecting the Master's invitation.

Why would anyone not want to come to such a feast? An excuse, you know, is just a lame, false reason that we give to try to cover up the REAL reason. What they all were trying to do was to please themselves without displeasing the man who had invited them. But it didn't work –believe me, he saw through their flimsy excuses, and he was furious! I understood.

But even in his anger, the Master knew what to do. There would be no wasting this feast, no sulking about those who had rejected the invitation – oh, no! He immediately called one of the other servants and told him to go out into the city streets and the alleys and invite the poor, the maimed, the halt, the blind – the outcast, the misfits, the beggars – he wanted them all – they were all welcome!

The servant quickly did as the Master had told him to do, and he had no trouble finding willing people to come. "Still there is room", the servant reported when he returned.

*"Well then go out to the highways and hedges and bring in complete strangers you find there, until my house is completely full!" Then turning toward me he said, "One thing is for sure, not one single person on the original guest list shall enjoy this banquet!" I was so glad that I was not one who had ignored his invitation. The opportunity had come and gone for them – the door was shut! Those that make the choice not to come to

the banquet when they can may be turned away when it's a "convenient" time for them!

So in they came – those who had been summoned by surprise! Just as the Master had wanted! The outcasts – the misfits – the broken – the needy – the forgotten! They were dirty – disheveled – destitute...faces forged with lines of pain, regret, shame and sin.

They hobbled in in silence – overwhelmed by the beauty and luxury of the banquet hall – barely daring to breathe!

There was the beggar I saw in the marketplace – the crippled boy who lives down the street – the old man with a crooked stick for a cane – the prostitute ashamedly attempting to wrap her scanty clothes more tightly to her body – the drunkard who staggered in from the back alley.

And now, the grace extended to them has made them rich – the mercy offered has made them welcome – accepted – children of the King!

And like children in a toy shop, they simply stared in awe at the splendor surrounding them.

One by one, we helped them to their seats – the candles glisten, the wine is poured – the fish is served.

Tears fill their eyes – you can almost read their minds.... "Is this really happening?" "Pinch me!" "When will I wake up and find it a dream?"

When they finally realized that they were not dreaming – this was real – they began to relax, look around a bit – and enjoy themselves. And my, how they ate! No doubt for many of them it was the first meal in a long time – the finest meal of a lifetime. Tears ran down my cheeks as I filled their plates and cut the bread and heard their laughter echo in my Master's house. It was truly the most joyful banquet ever!

The Master came alongside me while I was serving. Touching my arm he said, "Rachel, I want you to sit down, too. Come, sit right down here with me – this party is for you, too!"

"Oh no, Sir" I stammered. "I couldn't possibly. I'll eat later – these folks need me to..." But as I looked in his eyes, I knew his grace included me – as unthinkable and unfathomable as it was – it was true. I saw some of the other servants were already seated and so slowly, disbelievingly, I sat down too. To do otherwise would have broken my Master's heart.

"This is the way it will always be from now on," he said to everyone assembled. "This house – my house – this table – this must be the place where all are always welcome. This must be the place for publicans and sinners, for social outcasts of every sort. This must be the place for the hopeless and hurting –where all can come and eat and find acceptance, forgiveness and love. This must be a place where needs are met with my abundance!

You could have heard a pin drop. And then, people began to weep – to embrace one another

– to applaud the Master. I thought of the words of the prophet Isaiah – "Come, all you who are thirsty, come to the waters; and you who have no money, come, buy and eat! Come, buy wine and milk without money and without cost."

Come, come as you are friends. The Master invites you, too. His love, His mercy, His grace, His abundance is available! The table is spread – all things are now ready – COME!

SECTION III- PEOPLE JESUS MET

Chapter 9:

Mary of Bethany

(The Alabaster Box)

Texts: Luke 10: 38-42; John 11: 1, 5; Matthew 26: 7-13; Mark 14: 3-9; John 11:2, 12:3 (* Scripture quotes from The New Testament in Modern English – J.B. Phillips)

*P*erhaps it was a waste in some people's eyes – an inexcusable extravagance – but Jesus understood, and that's all that mattered to me.

I had to find some way that was uniquely my own to express my love for my Lord – that's why this alabaster box – this precious perfume.

I can remember the first time Jesus came to our little home in Bethany. He stopped to ask for a drink of water, and ended up staying for the evening meal around our table. He soon became a regular visitor – really like one of our family. He needed a refuge, He said – away from the pressing crowds – a quiet place, to simply rest.

I had gone with the crowds myself to hear him – often. Stood on the edge, and drank in every word He spoke – oh, but I tell you, the sweetest times of all were those evenings He came right into our home. His eyes were kind and loving, His words warm and tender. I could not leave His presence when He came – it was as though I were riveted in place. Dear Martha could not understand that. Her gift of hospitality pressed her to prepare the finest meals she could offer – with every amenity and accessory in its proper place. The Master loved her cooking – no doubt that is one of the reason He kept coming back! (One does get weary of fish and bread all the time, I am sure!) But sometimes, Martha put so much into her preparation that she spent all evening in the kitchen – and when the Master left, all she had to remember His visit by were her tired feet, and aching back!

I felt an urgency to sit at His feet – to take in His words – to just enjoy His presence! And when Martha scolded me for not doing my share in the kitchen, Jesus said that I had made the best choice, by being with Him. While Jesus surely enjoyed all that home cooking, He wanted Martha to know Him intimately, too. His words, I sensed, were immortal – life changing – heart stirring. His love was pure and genuine.

And then came the day when our brother Lazarus died. It was so sudden. We were stunned! He had been ill – and we sent for Jesus, but by the time He arrived, Lazarus had been dead four days! In our sorrow, we reached out to Jesus, and believed that He could make a difference.

"I am the resurrection, and the life", He said, "The one who believes in me will live, even though they die; and whoever lives by believing in me will never die. Do you believe this?" He asked. Of course we believed it! We believed that Lazarus would indeed rise again in the resurrection at the last day. Jesus had something very different in mind – and none of us were prepared for what He did next!

Jesus asked to go to the tomb where Lazarus was buried. Outside the tomb, He wept for the dear friend inside. Then He asked for the stone to be removed from the door of the tomb! Martha protested, thinking of the odor that would be inside from the decaying body. "Did I not tell you that if you believe, you will see the glory of God?" Jesus responded. So, the stone was removed! Jesus lifted His eyes heavenward, and prayed a brief prayer. When He finished praying, to everyone's astonishment, He called out in a loud voice – "Lazarus – come out!"

What? Come out? Lazarus brought back to life? Could it be? Was it possible? All time and eternity stood still as the hushed crowd waited to see what would happen next!

Shuffle-shuffle—shuffle –there was a sound – there was movement in the tomb – and suddenly – THERE STOOD LAZARUS IN THE DOORWAY – still bound in the grave clothes! A gasp went up from the crowd! I could not believe what I was seeing!

"Take off the grave clothes and let him go!" Jesus said. Oh, what joy to unravel those burying cloths, and welcome our brother back to the sun-light of God's love and life! Some people wept, some screamed, some murmured in disbelief, some stood in shocked silence. But as for Lazarus, Martha and me – we LAUGHED – all the way home!

What a miracle! The glory of God was revealed all right – in a resurrected body! Many more people turned to Jesus, and followed Him as a result of my brother's resurrection.

That was the reason for the feast – at the home of Simon the Leper. We had much to celebrate – much reason to honor Jesus. Simon, the FORMER leper, having his own cause to rejoice, offered his home for the celebration. Jesus came, along with many of His followers – and of course, Martha served! She spared no expense in providing a sumptuous banquet – the finest the Jerusalem marketplace could offer. How happy she was to give this gift to her Lord!

I had a gift, too. One that had cost a year's worth of wages to buy. My heart was pounding, as I brought it out from its hiding place. For a moment, I had second thoughts – maybe this was foolish. What I was about to do was out of place for a woman at such gatherings. Maybe I would only make a spectacle of myself, and not convey the deep love which motivated this outpouring! NO – I MUST do it – I WILL do it, I said to myself. Coming up behind Jesus, as He was reclining at the table, I broke the seal on the beautiful alabaster box of ointment – pouring the perfumed oil on His head. It ran down the folds of His seamless robe, and on to His feet. Quickly, I began to wipe away the excess with the hairs of my head, mingled with the tears that were now flowing freely down my face. The rich, pungent fragrance filled the whole room! Oh, I prayed that He would see deep into my heart, and know the magnitude of love that was there!

*Lost in my thoughts, I did not hear at first the scorn that was being hurled at me. "What is the point of such wicked waste?" Judas bemoaned – "Couldn't this perfume have been sold for a lot of money which could be given to the poor?" Others around the table began to agree with him, as they picked up the cry against me!

I lifted my tear-stained face to see the eyes of my Lord. The questions filled my mind. Couldn't these men understand? Didn't they see the shadow of a cross on the horizon? Couldn't they feel the cold winds of treachery and betrayal even across this table? Didn't they know that just this week, a special meeting of the Sanhedrin had been called, and they decided that Jesus must be put to death? Some were even seeking to kill Lazarus –it was because of his resurrection that many of the Jews were turning to Jesus. Jesus had told His followers plainly that He was going to die – they just did not understand it – they could not comprehend it. Were they blind and deaf?

*"Why must you make this woman feel uncomfortable?," Jesus spoke tenderly. "She has done a beautiful thing for me. You will have the poor with you always, but you will not always have me." Jesus turned to look at me – "When she poured this perfume on my body she was preparing it for my burial. I assure you that wherever the gospel is preached throughout the whole world, what she has done will also be told, as her memorial to me."

I was astounded. To think that simple act of love I had performed would be preserved and remembered – forever! I was seeking to honor Jesus – but He honored me!

The winds of adversity grew stronger, but the fragrance of mingled love remained. As the awful events of the week come to a climax, I watched in horror as my Lord was beaten – oh, so terribly beaten – almost beyond recognition – His beautiful face torn and swollen! He was spat upon, mocked and crowned with thorns – and yet, as He passed by on the Via Dolorosa, carrying His own cruel cross, I could still smell the perfume in His hair, and on His robe. I followed the sorry parade to Calvary – where they stripped Jesus, and tossed the anointed robe at the foot of the cross where the soldiers cast lots for it. In spite of the terrible stench of blood, sweat and death, certain winds carried to me the familiar fragrance of the oil, and Jesus, too, seemed comforted by that. Perhaps, as He labored to breathe while hanging on the cross, that perfume, and the love that had prompted its outpouring, comforted Him as He looked down upon those who tortured Him and said, "Father, forgive them, for they know not what they do!"

The alabaster box of Jesus' body was broken – His pure, sweet love was spilled out. A perfume more precious than anything in this world – so lovely – so truly extravagant! And still, it flows, down through the ages, and would be poured out upon every person – if they would only come to Him! My offering was nothing – NOTHING – pitiful compared to the outpouring of my Lord. And yet, He accepted it – He accepted ME! He loves me – and He poured out His life for me!

Oh, thank you, Jesus!

Chapter 10:

Mary of Magdala

**Texts: Matthew 15:39;Mark 16:9;
Luke 8:2-3;Matthew 27:56;Mark 15:40;
John 19:25; Matthew 27:61,28:1-7;
Mark 15:47, 16:1-7;Luke 23: 55,56, 24: 1-7;
John 20: 1, 11-13; Matthew 28: 8-10;
Mark 16:9; John 20:14-18**

*G*race beyond measure! Ah! I know first-hand the deepest meaning of those words because I experienced the marvelous grace of God from the very hand of Jesus Christ, my Lord.

Oh, but let us begin at the beginning. Magdala, my home town, was a bustling, thriving, town, nestled among the hills that stretched to the shores of the Sea of Galilee. Primitive textile factories and dye works added to its wealth, and made living affluent and secure. I grew up with more than the necessities of life – enjoying the comfort and pleasure of material substance. I soon learned, however, that though I came from a family of means, there were things that money simply could not buy!

At first, my parents thought it was a passing illness – a nervous maladjustment I would outgrow. Dragging me from physician to physician, they were determined to find a cure – to spare them the embarrassment of having a deranged, delusional daughter. Surely they had enough money – enough influence – they knew the right people. But as time went on, it became painfully clear to them that there WAS no cure – no turning the tide of the horrible possession that was overtaking my body, mind and soul.

Perhaps my parents were humiliated – perhaps they thought to put me away – I don't know, because all the while, I was becoming more and more oblivious to the needs and feelings of others around me. Actually, others around me were being afflicted, too. It seemed that all the forces of hell were loosed on earth when the Redeemer of the world walked among us. There was unbridled hate and evil in the human heart. Satan did his best to turn Jesus aside from His purpose and his legions of demons entered into many people of Jesus 'day to drive them into illness, torment and insanity. It is the darkest of all human misery – I know, because I was one of the victims!

Seven such demons of darkness thrashed about inside of me – gripping my will, perplexing my mind, numbing my heart. Growing stronger within me, they terrorized and convulsed my body until I had no will or reason, screaming insanely and ripping at my clothes. I was completely controlled, totally tormented, positively possessed by powers beyond my own – I was a slave!

I must have been a repulsive object to behold when Jesus came to me – disheveled – matted hair – vacant, glaring eyes – sunken cheeks – twisting and twitching, my body knew no rest!

But Jesus saw something in me that others did not. Into my living death He had come with the power of LIFE! With authority like no other, He commanded those tormenting demons to come out and stay out of me!

"Go back -, back to your hideous hell – you despicable evil spirits of the pit!" He ordered. One by one, the horrible hellions flew from me, seeing they had met their match, and I had met my Master! They HAD to flee – such evil could not co-exist with His love-His purity – His holiness!

His love illuminated the deep gloom of my heart, and soon spread through my entire being, and I passed from death into life – from darkness into His marvelous light! Jesus snatched me from the sure death of dread and despair, and in a moment made me a well woman. Peaceful – sane

– whole! Accepted, loved, and able to truly love in return!

He had done so much for me that I wanted to give every moment of my redeemed, reclaimed life to serve Him. All I wanted was to be near Jesus – there was nothing I would not do for Him. Overwhelming gratitude filled in all the places in my life that had once been so tortured. And so, with my back toward Magdala, I gladly left all, to follow Him!

I, along with other redeemed and healed women, accompanied Him everywhere. We gave from our means to supply the everyday needs of Jesus and the twelve. We did everything we could for their comfort and care.

To hear His teaching, to see His miracles, to feel His presence and power – this became my life – what I lived for – what I longed for! I had so much to be thankful for, that I could not forget, nor ever leave my Lord!

Then came the time for the greatest test of my love and devotion. The tide of popularity was turning – people were whispering – the Jewish leaders began aggressively seeking Jesus, trying with their questions to trap and accuse Him. It was blasphemy, they said, to call Himself the Son of God – to talk about God as His Father. Many thought Jesus had come to establish an EARTHLY Kingdom – to overthrow the Roman rule, and set up His own government. Even some of the disciples were waiting for Him to move in that direction. And, a few people believed He WAS who He said He was – the Messiah – the chosen One –" the Christ, the Son of the living GOD!" Thus, the people were divided and confused. It was the perfect time for the angry, jealous leaders to make their move!

His arrest happened in the garden – Gethsemane – one of His favorite places to go to talk to His Heavenly Father. He had just shared the Passover meal with His disciples, and they had retreated to the garden for prayer. Suddenly, the Roman guards appeared – with swords and spears and lanterns! It was one of the disciples – Judas, who betrayed Jesus with a kiss – insincere, cold – merely a sign to the soldiers as to who they should seize. No wonder Judas was so restless at supper – no wonder he ran from the upper room when Jesus announced – "One of you will betray me..."

Peter, in his usual awkward, spontaneous way, tried to defend Jesus. But alas, he simply proved he was better at fishing than at wielding a sword, and Jesus, without hesitation, healed one of the very ones who had come to seize and arrest Him!

Most of the twelve left Jesus that night – hiding in fear for their own lives. Confused, frustrated – and so afraid! But I heard it all – from the shadows – the mockery of a trial – the false accusations, the scourging and jeering. I felt the teeming anger of the crowd, fueled by the shouting jibes of the accusers. I saw the shuffling back and forth all during the night, until at last; Pilate was forced to make a decision.

By then, the crowd had become a violent mob, with only one thing on their minds as they screamed with raised fists – "Crucify Him...... Crucify Him!" It seemed like a terrible dream, and I wished I could awaken from it – but it was real!

Shoved through the streets by a walking sea of anger and turmoil, I, along with other women, followed Jesus with the jeering mob, through the appointed gate to Golgotha. We clung to each other and tried to comfort one another as the awful drama unfolded.

How I cringed with each blow of the hammer – still, I knew I could better stand to see His suffering than to be separated from Him. I saw everything – the soldiers with helmets and spears, laughing and mocking as they cast lots for the Savior's only earthly possession – His seamless robe. I shuddered when the tortured thief taunted Him from his own cross on the gruesome hill of death.

I heard His every word – "Father, forgive them..." "I thirst" – "It is finished!" – I felt the earth quake, and the hot winds blow – saw the darkness come around me like an ominous shroud. Jesus did not dismiss me from the cross, nor would I go away – I stayed until He died. I stayed until the Roman spear was thrust into His side, and watched as one by one the angry people left, their desire for blood satisfied. I stayed until Joseph and Nicodemus gently lifted His lifeless form from the cross. I stayed to wash His bloody body, and help to wrap it in clean linen. I watched as the two men carried His body into the borrowed tomb hewn out of the rock. I saw them as they rolled the great stone in front of the tomb, and then turned to go home. It was just three hours before the Sabbath.....but I stayed.

I so needed Him – was so lost without Him. I was reluctant to leave even His dead body. And so, I stayed – sitting beside the tomb – as long as I possibly could – I stayed!

The Sabbath was filled with thoughts of all my past encounters with Jesus. I loved Him so much as a person – Jesus meant everything to me! I loved Him for the peace and joy He had brought into my life, for the beauty of His perfect goodness and righteousness, for His tenderness and mercy – and oh, the GRACE! And for the glorious freedom and healing that grace had brought to me!

And so, very early the next morning – before dawn – I had to go back......there had not been enough time to properly prepare the body with spices and oil – it was the least I could do!

You cannot imagine my surprise when I arrived at the tomb and found the stone rolled away from the door! So many thoughts were racing through my mind as I ran to get Peter and John. They returned with me immediately, and found it to be as I had said. Who could have taken His body? Where did they put Him? Peter and John left as quickly as they had come – but I remained by the tomb, crying.

Through my tears, I stooped to look into the tomb again, and this time saw two angels – one at the head and one at the foot, where Jesus' body had been. They asked me why I was crying – "They have taken my Lord away, and I do not know where they have put Him!" I turned from the tomb in time to see the gardener standing there.

"Woman," he said tenderly, "why are you crying? Who is it you are looking for?"

Didn't everyone know this was Jesus' grave? Didn't everyone feel my pain? "Sir, if you have carried Him away, tell me where you have put Him, and I will get Him!"

"Mary" He said – Mary – only One Person spoke my name with such love and deep compassion. Could it be – my tears had blurred my vision – but there was no mistaking that voice! "Master!" I cried – and ran to embrace Him. I wanted to hold Him to this earth, so He would never leave again.

"Do not hold on to me," He said, "for I have not yet ascended to the Father."

It seemed like a rebuke – but I know now that I needed to learn that I must assume a deeper, spiritual relationship with Jesus – that He would be with me in a spiritual way always –"even unto the end of the world"!

"Go instead to my brothers and tell them,' I am ascending to my Father and your Father – to my God and your God!' "

He commissioned ME to be the first messenger of the resurrected Lord! Trembling with astonishment and joy, I flew to bring the glorious news of hope and life to the mourning disciples! No woman ever ran to deliver a more triumphant message than I did! What a privilege was mine to be the first bearer of such news! The last to leave the cross – the first at the empty tomb – the resurrected Lord appeared to ME – first of all! It was proof to me that no depth of sin – no possession of devils even, shall separate us from the love of Christ. That His forgiveness and love overcome everything! Only love Him simply –sincerely - completely as do I – and He will come to YOU also! He will call you by your name – He will employ you in His service – by His Grace – His GRACE BEYOND MEASURE!

Chapter 11:

Jared's Lunch

(And the mother who packed it!)

**Text: Matthew 14: 15-21;
Mark 6: 35-44; Luke 9: 12 – 17**

**John 6: 1 – 66 ;(Any quotes from this
portion are from The New Testament in
Modern English -J.B.Phillips) Psalm 34:8**

T was preparing the evening meal outdoors over an open fire. It had been a quiet day. Joel had been gone since before daybreak in his little fishing boat. Rebekah had been playing with Sarah and Rachel from across the street most of the day – and Jared, that mischievous lad of mine, had begged me to pack his lunch so he could hike off to the hillside. He had heard it murmured about town that Jesus – the teacher from

Nazareth – was going to be coming around, with His followers, too.

Almost a mass exodus, it was – scores of people left Tiberius and made their way to the hillsides. Shops closed, houses emptied as whole families trekked off! It was really kind of strange and unsettling. Hardly anyone was afoot. Seems like such a fuss made about this stranger of Galilee.

I was reluctant to let Jared go with such a crowd, but he does have a way of begging and pleading which breaks down my defenses. Besides, our friend Nathaniel the coppersmith and his wife Elizabeth were going, and I knew they would look after him.

Ah, but Jared is ALWAYS hungry – at that age where we just cannot fill him up! I knew he would surely be famished after that hike to the grassy slopes. Well, a good fisher-wife always has some fish around – small ones not fit to go to the marketplace. So, I quickly packed his lunch sack with two fish and five small barley loaves left over from the day before. Not much of a lunch, really – but enough to keep him from starving. I could likely have added some cheese and figs if he would have given me more time. Oh, but he was so excited he just snatched the bag out of my hand, kissed me lightly on the cheek, and was off like an antelope – bounding across the yard and out the gate before I could turn around! Boys! Always out for adventure – hiding behind rocks and exploring caves. ALL boy, he is – that Jared.

A few had stopped by the gate as I stood watching Jared disappear into the crowd. They invited me to join the procession. Humph! Not I – trekking off to see a man I did not know – and the things I heard about Him made me wonder. Harmless enough, I supposed Him to be – but strange in His teachings and ways. I had heard He performed some miracles though, and that DID make me more than a bit curious – but still, not enough to give up a quiet day at home. I had many things planned – washing, sweeping, mending, cooking – maybe even a moment or two just to sit and daydream or drift off to sleep a bit!

The hours passed quickly, and I did accomplish much – but now and again I would stop and scan the horizon – far across the Sea of Galilee – and wonder what Jared might be seeing or hearing from that Jesus. Perhaps I should have gone, too. I thought, "Next time He comes, I will go – I will!"

I felt guilty, disappointed, scared and excited – all at the same time. It seemed as though I could not stop thinking about what might be happening on the other side of the lake. I was shaken from my thoughts as Jared suddenly bolted through the gate. He was breathless and wide-eyed.

"Mother – mother – they want to make Him king – there were hundreds of people – and no one thought about eating – and then Jesus took my lunch and it fed everybody there – and here are some leftovers to prove to you and father! It was a miracle, mother! Oh mother, do come with me – I want to go back and hear more – mother !"

"Hold on, Jared" I said. "Sit yourself down here under the tree, catch your breath awhile, and then start at the beginning."

Just then Joel came home from his day on the lake. I called to him to join Jared and me in the cool evening shade. I wanted him to hear what Jared was saying.

"Oh mother – father – Jesus is wonderful! You must hear Him, too!"

"Son, tell us what happened", Joel said

"Well, mother had prepared a little lunch for me to take up the mountain– she knew I would get hungry, being gone all day, and in the outdoors like that. To tell you the truth, I forgot all about the lunch by the time I got to where Jesus was. There were hundreds of people there – thousands – from all over the Decapolis. He touched many people and healed them – and Jesus' words were – well, they were comforting and kind. I felt as though He was speaking just to me, and there was no one else around."

Jared went on to tell us that time went quickly. No one even thought about taking time to eat anything. Then Jesus had mentioned something about food to His followers, and Jared had remembered his lunch! He would gladly share his lunch with Jesus; he had told Andrew when he came through the crowd looking for food of any sort. So it seems Andrew marched our Jared right up to Jesus! "There is a boy here who has five barley loaves and a couple of fish, but what's the good of that for such a crowd?" Jared had said there were about 5000 men there, plus women and children. Then Jesus had everyone sit down – there are many grassy places in those hills. He took Jared's little lunch, and when He gave thanks, He gave it to His followers to give to the people. What happened next is unbelievable, but true. Jesus used Jared's lunch to feed everyone there – not just a crumb or a taste – He fed them until they could not eat any more! As long as there were hungry people, there was fish and bread! In fact, when everyone had eaten all they wanted, Jesus had His followers gather the fragments that remained – and there were twelve basketsful! Besides, Jared's little lunch bag was bulging – twice the size it had been that morning when I packed it!

Joel and I sat in silent awe and amazement to think Jared had been a part of such a miracle!

The silence was shattered by the buzzing sound of many voices, and the crunch of many feet on the pebbled streets. People were coming to our gate – friends, strangers – people from towns far away. They were shouting about Jared's lunch – about the miraculous feeding – but mostly about Jesus and how surely He had come to be our king!

He would free us from the bondage of Rome. Ah, it was a high-spirited crowd – looking as though they had already been liberated! Their joy was absolutely contagious!

Would we come with them, they asked – back to the other side of the lake – to see Jesus – to hear Him again – would we come along?

Joel and I looked at each other, and without hesitation, together we shouted, "Yes – Yes – YES!"

"Some of you can go across in my fishing boat with us," Joel was saying – while I was tending to the cooking fire and making sure Rebekah would be looked after. There was no keeping Jared home, of course. In minutes we had gathered up a cloak or two and set sail with a mixed array of passengers for the eastern shore. My heart was fairly pounding within me. The less than gentle tossing of the boat back and forth awakened me to the reality that darkness had long since overtaken us, and we were also in somewhat of a storm. Something else was happening on the lake, but we pressed on – taking much longer than usual to cross, for we were straining at the oars to keep on course.

At last, we safely reached the shore, and found some grassy places to rest and sleep until daybreak came, and we could look for Jesus. It was a long night for me – sleep would not come, for I had much anticipation for the morrow!

As soon as the sun broke over the lake, the people gathered to look for Jesus – but He was not to be found. Other boats arrived from Tiberius –and so it was decided that we would go to Capernaum – Jesus must be there!

So across to the north shore we went – wondering how Jesus got there during the night – for He had sent His followers away in their boat, and He himself had retreated further up the mountain for prayer, we learned. Nevertheless, we found Him at last – at the synagogue in Capernaum.

"When did you come here, Rabbi?" someone asked Him immediately. That was not important to me - for I was still filled with the wonder of His miracles, and the hope of what His coming might mean for all of us.

Jesus got right to the heart of the matter. "Believe me", replied Jesus, "when I tell you that you are looking for me now not because you saw my signs but because you ate that food and had all you wanted. You should not work for the food which does not last but for the food which lasts on into eternal life. This is the food the Son of Man will give you, and He is the one who bears the stamp of God the Father."

This made them ask Him, "What must we do to carry out the work of God?"

Jesus said, "The work God wants you to do, is to believe in the One whom He has sent to you."

People began to understand that Jesus was talking about Himself – so the grumbling began –

"Then what sign can you give us that will make us believe in you? What work are you doing? Our forefathers ate manna in the desert just as the scripture says, 'He gave them bread out of heaven to eat.' "

Jesus said, "That is true indeed, but what matters is not that Moses gave you bread from Heaven, but that my Father is giving you the true bread from Heaven. For the bread of God which comes down from Heaven gives life to the world."

"Lord, please give us this bread, now and always!" many shouted all together.

Then Jesus said it clearly – "I myself am the bread of life. The man who comes to me will never be hungry, and the man who believes in me will never be thirsty. Yet I have told you that you have seen me and do not believe. Everything that my Father gives me will come to me and I will never refuse anyone who comes to me..... Everyone who sees the Son, and trusts in Him should have eternal life....."

I looked around at that crowd, and I could tell the Jewish leaders were more than skeptical – and they began to murmur. "Is this not Jesus – the son of Joseph, whose parents we know? How can He now say 'I have come down from Heaven'?"

And they began to laugh and make jest of it among themselves. The mood was changing. Jesus knew their thoughts and whisperings.

"Do not grumble among yourselves," He said. "I myself am the bread of life" He repeated. "Your fathers ate manna in the desert, and they died – I myself am the living bread which came down from Heaven, and if anyone eats this bread he will live forever. The bread which I will give is my own body and I shall give it for the life of the world."

A wave of disbelief swept through the crowd – murmurs turned to taunts and shouts – many quarrels erupted. "How can this man give us his body to eat?"

One by one, many people began to turn away from Jesus – these were hard sayings which they could not understand or believe – nor could they follow Him anymore.

They, seeing, still could not believe – yet somehow in my heart, I felt it should be the opposite – that if I would BELIEVE, I would SEE and understand in my heart.

Joel drew alongside of me, and took my hand. "We must believe, Lydia," he said to me. "I do not yet fully understand, but there is something compelling here –something drawing me – we must not turn back!"

I squeezed his hand – "It's true, my dear Joel," I said, "I cannot explain all that He has said, nor my response to it – but I must follow – I MUST!" Jared, too, in his childlike faith, reached out to Jesus.

Who knows where our walk will take us? Who knows what it will cost? Still, I believe He IS the source of life – eternal life – and that by bringing Him into the very center of our lives we thus "partake" of Him.

Oh, there is much to learn – I am yet feeble in my faith – but I am hungering for Him – for this living bread – and I shall be fed! As He multiplied Jared's lunch to feed the thousands – so will He feed me – over and over again as I give up my little "all" to Him. Little is much, when you give it to God, you know! And this bread – this living bread is for all generations – yours as well as mine.

As the Psalmist said, "Oh taste, and see that the Lord is good!"

Today we return to our humble home – with winged feet, happy hearts, and satisfied souls – more than ever before because of the Bread who came down from Heaven! Oh taste – taste and see!

Loaves And Fishes

SECTION IV- LENT AND EASTER

Chapter 12:

Claudia Procula

(Pilate's Wife)

Texts: Matthew 27: 11-31

My dream still haunts me. You can't imagine how real it seemed!

And it all happened – just as I saw it – the cruel mob, the crucified men, darkness engulfing the land, the earthquake – even the veil in the temple torn from top to bottom. I am still trembling!

I've felt so many different emotions these past few days. Less than a week ago I stood on the flat roof of the palace and watched this man called Jesus enter the city of Jerusalem. He rode a young donkey, and was surrounded by palm-waving Galileans. Their song of triumph could be heard in all the streets – "Hosanna – Blessed is he who comes in the name of the Lord!"

It was the first time I had ever seen Him – though I had wanted to for many months. As He passed by, He looked up, as if He knew I was up there watching for Him. Our eyes met for such a brief moment – but I shall never forget it.

I have followed Him this week – wherever I could – disguised so no one would recognize me as Claudia Procula, wife of the Roman Governor.

The day after His entrance into the city, I heard Him teaching in the temple court. I hid behind one of the pillars and heard Him speak many parables. The mood of Jerusalem seemed to be changing from one of festivity and joy to that of unrest and tension.

The Pharisees and Sadducees were clearly perturbed by the masses that followed Jesus – by the authority with which He spoke – the profound effect His teaching had on all who listened. He spoke about impending judgment and destruction – but also about coming glory and resurrection! He talked with such confidence about the future – as if He'd already <u>been</u> there. He seemed to read my mind and answer all the questions I had about life and death. The religious leaders scorned and questioned Him – but He responded with words about loving the Lord our God with all our heart, mind, soul and strength – and our neighbor as ourselves. It seemed I could not get enough of His teachings!

Then last night, Jesus took His closest followers into an upper chamber for the Passover meal – and no one but His chosen disciples could join Him there.

All evening as Pilate and I sat by the fireside, I wondered to myself what was going on in that upper room – what wonderful words was He saying? What acts of love and kindness was He bestowing upon these men – His most intimate band of followers and friends?

My reverie was rudely interrupted when the High Priests appeared at our door and requested a special detachment of soldiers to arrest Jesus!

Arrest Him? For what? For loving and healing? For teaching and forgiving? It made no sense to me! Oh, I had heard some clamor among the people, and there was the mounting tension among the religious leaders in particular – but arrest Him? It couldn't possibly be!

I waited for several hours – but heard nothing. At last I decided to try to get some sleep.

But restful sleep was never to come.

I tossed fitfully upon my ivory couch, my mind filled with fear for the future!

I was afraid of what might be happening to Jesus – but I was also keenly aware of the different problems facing my husband. Pilate hates the Jews, but he also fears them. He is at their mercy and they know it!

Then there was the concern about his personal danger from the anger of Caesar – if a rebellion should break out in consequence of the arrest and possible imprisonment of Jesus.

I was deeply troubled in spirit – and awoke frequently drenched in perspiration – cold and clammy from the vivid visions I was experiencing.

It was the longest night of my life! At daybreak I quickly arose and discovered Pilate had already left. In the halls I heard muted murmurings about a "trial before Pilate" – "an angry mob" – "Jesus the Christ"

I hurried to bathe and dress – I must get a message to Pilate before it's too late! Still reeling from the awful scenes that had passed before me during the night – I stumbled along the corridors to a small window overlooking "the Pavement" – Pilate's judgment seat would be there in the court yard. The Jews would not enter the Governor's Palace – not on this Sabbath eve day – lest by entering a heathen dwelling they would have defiled themselves and been debarred from further participation in the festival activities. Thus, Pilate was forced to come forth, with no good grace, to hear their complaint.

Quickly I scrawled a note, and gave it to one of the servants to take to Pilate.

"Don't have anything to do with that innocent man, for I have suffered a great deal today in a dream because of Him."

It seemed as if my dream had called upon me to stand as an intercessor for a man I knew to be just.

I can still see Him standing there in the Judgement Hall– condemned, forsaken, betrayed. The first rays of the morning sun were resting in benediction upon His head as He stood silent before His accusers.

His piercing, yet compassionate eyes moved across the crowd – and as Pilate's question echoed through the chambers, it seemed to be one that we all must answer personally – "What shall I do then with Jesus who is called Christ?"

Yes, what shall I do with Him – it was as though I had to make that decision for myself.

My voice was so small

My plea, so feeble.

I was overcome by a terrible sense of failure as the dread visions of the night were reenacted before my eyes.

The wild cries "Crucify Him – Crucify Him!" chilled me to the bone, and raged around the ears of Pilate as if the sea were tossed to tempest and he were a mere shell in the midst of the waves.

Pilate tried to appease them – he had Him scourged – mocked Him – allowed the soldiers to crown Him with thorns and spit upon Him. "Here is your King!" Pilate appealed to their compassion, as Jesus again stood pale and bleeding before them. Surely that sight must soften them.

They howled like wolves a thirst for blood – "Take Him away – take Him away! – Crucify Him!"

"Shall I crucify your King?" Pilate asked.

"We have no King but Caesar!"

And poor, poor Pilate had not the courage to do justice!

Pilate has gone to that basin and washed his hands a hundred times – and still there is no cleansing for his sin – no peace from the struggles within – no release from his guilt.

And yet, I somehow feel that if even now we joined the others at the foot of that cross – if even now we beheld His dying form – His eyes of love and mercy would look upon us – and we would be forgiven.

Oh Pilate – my dear tormented husband – won't you come with me now – I believe it is the only cure for your broken soul!

Oh, but alas! His stubborn pride – his position – his fear of the people and the emperor – they bind him like fetters and keep him from doing what perhaps even in his own heart he knows he needs to do!

What foolish things keep us from following! This luxury – these things all seem so unimportant to me now. There is one burning desire within my heart – to know HIM – to love HIM – to serve HIM all my days!

But now, it's too late.........or is it?

Chapter 13:

"I've Just Seen Jesus!"

(Salome)

Texts: John 1:29; Matthew 5: 1-12; Matthew 5-7; Matthew 20: 20-28; Mark 15:40, 16:1,2; Matthew 20: 18,19, 28:1-10

James – John – James – John – Where are you?

Come – come quickly! You must go to Galilee – JESUS IS ALIVE! He said He'll meet you there! James – John!

Have YOU seen them – my sons, James and John? I must find them, and tell them the great news – HE LIVES! JESUS LIVES!

James – John – Oh, where could they be?

All of His disciples left Him, you know – except for my John who was there at the cross until the end – faithful, he was!

Ah, I remember so well when James and John first came to tell me about Jesus – they had been following John the Baptizer – listening to his prophecies of a coming Messiah. I could not help but be curious myself as they shared his messages with me. Then, one day, when they went out to see John – a stranger was with him – one my sons did not recognize.

"Look, the Lamb of God", John had said, "Who takes away the sin of the world!" James and John were moved by the compassion and character of this stranger. "He is the One Mother," they insisted. "Come along with us – see Him – hear Him for yourself! He is truly God's anointed One!"

Well, before I could get to Him – He came to us – walking the shores between our fleet of fishing boats – talking with our servants. Our sons knew Him immediately. He spoke their names and said simply – "Follow Me!" At once, they laid down their nets – and followed Him. I saw the whole thing as I sat by the window in our home by the Sea of Galilee.

"What do you make of it?" I asked Zebedee that night during our evening meal. "Have our sons acted foolishly – leaving the security of their occupation as fishermen? Surely they know the business will one day be theirs – why would they just walk away – and leave it all behind?"

Zebedee said nothing for the longest while – he just looked out the window toward the place where Jesus had passed earlier that day. Finally, he spoke.

"Salome," he said softly – "I would have followed Him myself if He had spoken my name! I cannot explain it – there is something compelling in His voice – something loving in His touch – something magnetic in His eyes. One could respond no other way than with obedience! No, my dear" he said tenderly, "our sons have not acted foolishly – they have responded to a holy calling – they have lost themselves in a cause far greater than catching fish and earning a living!" And then he continued, with deep conviction, "Salome, this man is the One we've all been waiting for – I am convinced He is Messiah – the Promised One – our Redeemer! We must hear Him, too – we must learn all we can from Him!"

My heart pounded with joy and excitement. "Really Zebedee? The Messiah? The Promised one? Where can we go to see and hear Him ourselves?"

"He teaches in the Decapolis" Zebedee said, "ask the servants to get the news from the market-place. It will be noised about when He is coming our way!"

A few days later, Rebekah, one of my hand-maids came running breathlessly, saying she had just seen this Jesus coming through the Valley of Doves – just across the lake.

A great crowd of people followed Him. I ran to tell Zebedee – and we took one of our smaller boats over to the other shore, and joined the multitude that had now assembled on the grassy slope. People in the crowd were sharing stories of how Jesus had healed many who were sick among them – even paralytics and those who were demon-possessed. People had gathered from many towns in the province to hear His word that day!

Suddenly, a strong voice spoke so all could hear.

"Blessed are the poor in spirit," He said, "For theirs is the Kingdom of Heaven. Blessed are those who mourn – for they shall be comforted. Blessed are the pure in heart – for they will see God! Blessed are the peacemakers – for they shall be called the sons of God!"

He spoke out boldly against murder, adultery, divorce and judging others. In fact, He said we should not point out the splinter in someone else's eye, when we are walking around with a beam sticking out of our own eye! He told us to love our enemies – to do good to those who persecute us. He told us not to worry about what we would eat or drink – or the clothes we would wear. He said our Heavenly Father knows we have need of all these things. Instead, we should seek His Kingdom FIRST, and then everything else we need will be supplied! He taught plainly about prayer, love and the true way to God's Kingdom. He taught with such compassion and conviction. His touch could heal the lame, the blind, the diseased – but He also cast out demons – and forgave

SINS! Whoever came to Jesus was changed – dramatically!

It was astonishing – for He spoke with the authority of God – and everyone knew it!

From that time on – Zebedee and I followed Him everywhere – we supported His ministry in every way we could. He often used our fishing boats, and we even bought a small house for Him to use in Capernaum. He had nothing of His own in this world – at least that gave Him some place to rest when He wasn't off to Judea or one of the other provinces.

Ah! There was a new day dawning for all of Palestine – one could almost TASTE it! Jesus spoke often about His Kingdom – surely it would not be long before He would overthrow the Roman rule, and we could be our own people once again!

I was so proud of my boys for becoming His followers! They weren't just "numbered with the twelve" – they were both part of the inner circle – those closest to Jesus. He often asked just Peter and my James and John to accompany Him to some special healing – or some other intimate event in His life. They were with Him constantly! "The sons of Thunder" Jesus called them – they were so outspoken and strong.

As Jesus' fame and popularity spread, the Pharisees and other Jewish leaders became more and more angered. The people became more and more divided – those who dearly loved and followed Jesus – and those who bitterly hated and denounced Him! His hand was going to have to move soon to establish His Kingdom!

One day, on the way to Jerusalem, the Master called His disciples off to the side of the road, and told them when they reached the city that He was going to be betrayed, and sentenced to death. He would be mocked, tortured and crucified – and on the third day, He would be raised up alive!

Jesus so often spoke in parables and picture language – no one really knew what this meant – but I felt it was a sign that His Kingdom was at hand, and I wanted my sons to have the places of honor in His Kingdom!

I moved out of the crowd, and knelt before Jesus.

"What is it you want?" Jesus asked – and I made my bold request.

"Grant that one of these two sons of mine may sit at your right and the other at your left in your kingdom."

He paused for a moment, and looked deep within my eyes. "You don't know what you are asking," He said. Turning to James and John He said, "Can you drink the cup I am going to drink?"

"We can!" they responded.

"You will indeed drink from my cup," He said. Then turning again to me He said, "But to sit at my right or left is not for me to grant. These places belong to those for whom they have been prepared by my Father."

Then looking at the band of disciples He said, "Whoever wants to become great among you, must be your servant, and whoever wants to be first, must be your slave- just as the Son of Man did not come to be served, but to serve, and to give his life as a ransom for many."

I was so ashamed! Jesus had rebuked me tenderly, but firmly. Why had I been so ambitious for my sons? It was all so confusing. What really WAS Jesus' mission to us?

When we got to the city, everything happened just as Jesus had tried to tell us along the road. At first, He was received joyfully into Jerusalem. The people praised and honored Him! The Pharisees were infuriated, and obviously plotted day and night to trap and arrest Him. Jesus spoke out in open condemnation of the Pharisees – calling them "Hypocrites" – "blind guides" – "serpents" and a "brood of vipers!" The atmosphere grew more tense and hostile.

Near the end of the week, He met with His disciples for an intimate observance of the Passover meal. He spoke again of His death and ultimate resurrection. And then, James and John told me that Jesus rose from the table, laid aside His outer garments, and girded Himself with a towel. He then proceeded to wash the feet of each and every disciple around the table!

Jesus – the Master – the Messiah – stooped to wash their feet! Truly He HAD come to be a servant – lowly, humbly doing the will of God, His Father.

Later that night, it was one of the twelve, Judas Iscariot, who betrayed his Master – into the hands of sinners! Jesus was roughly shuffled back and forth, all night, between Caiaphas, Herod and Pilate. It was finally Pilate, the Roman Procurator, who delivered Jesus over into the hands of the people!

I could not believe how they treated Him – beating – spitting – slapping – mocking – laughing – taunting and joking all the while! Where were His followers? Where were those who loved and believed in Him? Would no one come to His defense? It was awful! SO many times I wanted to scream – "Stop!" "Enough!" The crowd had gone MAD! And yet – it seemed to be unfolding just as Jesus said it would!

I soon found myself being jostled in the crowd – carried along on the road to Golgotha – a place of execution. In numb disbelief, I stood at the edge of the crowd watching in horror, as Jesus was nailed to a cross, and lifted in shame for all to see Him die an agonizing death!

Through my tears, as I looked at Him there, my eyes were drawn to two other figures – one on the right hand, and one on the left – they were dying with Him. Suddenly, I remembered my foolish request for my sons- "One on the right hand, and one on the left, Lord, when you come into your Kingdom". This is the cup Jesus spoke of! I saw it clearly now!

I fell on my knees, so deeply moved by this Servant who was giving His life for me!

"O God, make ME a servant – give me a servant heart!" I prayed.

Soon it was over – darkness descended – Jesus was dead. Hope was gone – gloom and despair filled the heart of every believer and follower. The other women and I had done so little to help Jesus. We could not speak before the High Council in His defense – we could not appeal to Pilate – we could not stand up against the crowds – we couldn't overpower the Roman guards. We DID stay at the cross – we DID follow His body to the tomb – and now, this morning, there was one last act of kindness and love we COULD do!

There was just a faint flicker of hope as the words He had spoken played over and over again in my mind – "My Kingdom is not of this world" He had said. "The third day, I will rise again!"

Could it be? Dare I believe? That hope was pounding within me this morning on the way to the tomb. We were going to prepare and anoint His body – there had not been time before the Sabbath. As we came into the garden, talking among ourselves about who would roll away the great stone from the door of the tomb, we suddenly saw that the tomb was already open – the stone was already rolled back – the place where He laid was empty – and the tomb was filled with Heavenly light! An angel spoke to us!

"Do not be afraid", he said, "I know that you are looking for Jesus, who was crucified. He is not here ; He has risen, just as He said! Come and see the place where He lay. Then – go quickly – and tell His disciples: ' He is risen from the dead and is going ahead of you into Galilee...' "

Oh, I tell you, we RAN from that tomb – frightened, excited, amazed – too overwhelmed with wonder to speak to each other. Then, as we were making our way back here to find the disciples – Jesus HIMSELF appeared in the road – "Greetings!" He said.

We fell on our knees and worshiped Him – embracing His feet, as if to hold Him down from ever leaving us again!

"Do not be afraid" He told us – "Go tell my brothers to go to Galilee; there they will see me."

I've just seen Jesus – I tell you, HE'S ALIVE! HE'S ALIVE FOREVERMORE! Oh, I just want to be His servant – it is the only honor I will ever need!

He's alive – James!—John! Where are you boys? James! John! Come quickly!

Why do you seek the living among the dead. He is not here, but has risen." Luke 24:5-6

Chapter 14:

Dinner Guest in Emmaus

(Wife of Cleopas)

Texts: John 8: 2-59, 9:1-41; Luke 24:13-35

I am glad you came today – I have much to tell you! Come in – come in!

These days have been incredible for Cleopas and me – I hardly know where to begin – but I MUST tell you! It's about Jesus!

Oh, I have been thinking today about the first time I saw Him – I shall never forget it. It was the Feast of the Tabernacles and everyone was in Jerusalem for the celebration.

I was in the market place when news came that Jesus was in the temple, teaching. No one had really expected Him to come – there was much unrest and division among the people about His message and miracles – those Scribes and Pharisees in particular, were just looking for ways to trap Him! And that day, they brought to Him a woman caught in the very act of adultery. They asked Jesus to support the Law of Moses and sanction their stoning of the woman! But I heard Jesus just ignored their trick question and stooped down to write something in the sand. They pressed Him for an answer – so He stood up and said, "Let any one of you who is without sin be the first to throw a stone at her." Then they said He stooped down and wrote some more. I wish I knew what He wrote – maybe it was people's names in the crowd – or maybe He wrote some of the sins THEY had committed. Whatever it was – it worked! And one by one, those accusers dropped the stones they had in their hands and left without saying another word! No one was left to condemn the woman – and Jesus told her He did not condemn her either, and she was to go, and sin no more!

Well, I guess that confrontation caused quite a discussion among the Jewish leaders, and when He referred to God as His Father, they took up stones to throw at HIM. But I understand Jesus just walked right through the midst of them, unharmed.

That's when I saw Him – I was standing just outside the temple gate, talking to my blind friend Marcus, when Jesus came by. He had such love in His eyes as He looked at Marcus – I could just tell that He loved him. But then, He did a strange thing. He spat on the ground, and then picked up the moistened clay, and placed it on Marcus's eyes. "Go, wash in the pool of Siloam" Jesus said – and Marcus went off obediently. A crowd had quickly gathered, and when I turned back from watching Marcus, Jesus was gone.

Next thing I knew, Marcus, who had been born blind – came back from the pool declaring he could SEE! He was like a little child, in awe of everything he was seeing for the first time! It was truly a miracle!

Oh – But those Pharisees – they were all up in arms, because it was the Sabbath, and they started questioning Marcus and his parents and friends.

I had to leave then – but I felt such a glow in my heart from having met Jesus. My life just wasn't the same after that! I kept thinking about that tender look of love for Marcus, and somehow I felt that Jesus must love everyone with that same kind of love!

My husband, Cleopas, and his brother Benjamin became followers of His. They even made a trip or two to the Galilee and saw some of the miracles He did around Capernaum.

I tell you, Jesus made a change in our lives – in our home. Cleopas became more tolerant and patient – and I certainly became more caring and forgiving. Even though I had a household to keep together, I went to hear His teaching every time I could.

But the trouble in Jerusalem just wouldn't stop. Every time I went to the market place, I heard people talking of the mounting hatred against Jesus, and I began to fear for His life!

It was time for the Passover Celebration. The 7 miles from Emmaus to Jerusalem was crowded with travelers and people coming from all around for the festivities. Some of my family was coming up from Jericho, and I was very busy with many preparations for extra people in our little home. It was a sacred time, and a very joyful time.

I could hardly believe my ears when, in the middle of all of our celebrating, I learned that Jesus had been arrested. I think all Jerusalem was awake and troubled that night – certainly no one slept at our house! Word came to us throughout the night from neighbors, or from Jonathan, the shepherd boy. It seems Jesus was being put through some sort of mock trial – between Herod, Caiaphas, and Pilate, the Roman Governor. Surely everything will be all right, we thought. Jesus was always more than able to hold His own against the Jewish leaders. Still, our hearts were filled with anxiety.

Just before dawn, our nephew Stephen came sobbing to our door. Stephen is a vinegar boy – he has charge of the vinegar at executions – giving it to the criminals to help numb their pain. Between sobs he told us he had been notified to prepare for an execution of 3 men.....Thaddeus Bar Jonah, a known robber, Thomas Bar Jacob – a thief and possible murderer – and Jesus Bar Joseph.....Jesus! Not my Jesus? Not Jesus of Nazareth? It could not be! This man who had healed the sick, raised the dead, calmed the wind and the waves, fed the multitudes – this Jesus who taught us about ourselves and our need for forgiveness and love from God our Father – this wonderful man was now going to die as a common criminal – why? What wrong had He done? What crime had He committed? No one seemed to know....not even the ones who had sentenced Him to die!

The day dawned with steel gray skies, clouds hanging low and ominous. I could not concentrate on anything at home, and so we went up to Jerusalem to try to learn more about these unbelievable events.

By the time we arrived, crowds had already gathered on either sides of the narrow main street. Some women were already weeping, their bodies convulsing with emotion. Soon there came around the corner a pale, bleeding man I barely recognized, staggering beneath the weight of the heavy Roman cross. His face was swollen – blood ran down His cheeks from the crown of thorns pressed into His brow. I blinked back hot tears as my heart pounded within me. "Why? Why God is this happening? Why don't you do something?"

Then Jesus passed right in front of us – and I swear to you, despite the pain and agony He was experiencing, He looked at us with that same tenderness I had seen in His eyes toward Marcus, my blind friend– a deep, deep love that seemed to say "I am doing this for you!" I could not explain it, but that is what I saw and felt!

Flanked by soldiers and cursing rebels, we followed the procession outside the city walls to Golgotha – God-forsaken place that it is – nothing more than a garbage dump. Such an unfitting place for the Holy, Pure One! Why, oh why was He there? It didn't make any sense. We watched in horror as they nailed Him to the cross He had struggled to carry. We saw Him writhe with pain as the cross was lifted, and then dropped into place, and His flesh tore on those nails. Oh, it was awful!

I couldn't stand to look on Him like this – it was too horrible – I had to go home. Yet, even as I turned to leave His eyes met mine once more – I saw again that same look of love – and then I heard Him say the most astounding thing! "Father," He said, "forgive them, for they know not what they do!"

It was, I think, the longest day of my life – and when Cleopas returned that evening, he had reports of darkened skies, an earthquake – resurrected bodies – and the bizarre rending of the temple veil. He told me Stephen had been there to try to comfort Jesus – but Jesus refused the vinegar – and that at about 3:00, Jesus had died!

I tell you, sorrow filled our hearts. We could not speak of it – sleep would not come – no one ate. A thick cloud of disappointment and dread hung over our home like a shroud. Hours became days, with no move on our part to return to normalcy.....it seemed inappropriate.

And then – this morning – Stephen came again, this time stammering with excitement! Some women had gone to Jesus' tomb to anoint His body. Seems the stone had been rolled away from the door of the tomb – and the body was gone! Some were saying He had arisen from the dead! Oh, but that was just hearsay!

Nevertheless, Cleopas and Benjamin decided to go into the city to check it out for themselves. I stayed behind to prepare a meal I was sure they would be ready for upon their return from Jerusalem. All day, I wanted to dare to believe – but I just couldn't. I had seen Him on that cross – yes, He was dead – no doubt about that. I paced the floor, cried and prayed – for hours.

It was getting dusk when I heard the familiar footsteps on the threshold. My heart leaped within my breast! At last – some news! But, what was this ? A stranger was with them. Who was he-someone who had joined them on the way home? Seems this stranger was not aware of all the events of the past few days, so Cleopas and

Benjamin told him all about it – and then he had told them....told them how this was all part of God's plan – really from the beginning – through all the prophecies of the Old Testament. They were so enthralled with this stranger that they invited him to stay the night with us, so they could talk some more with him.

Well, I was glad to hear, too – and happy I had some hungry men to enjoy the meal I had prepared.

And then suddenly, that meal became unlike any other we had ever had! The stranger took the warm bread I had just baked, blessed it, and broke it to share with us! Oh, I tell you, there was something so familiar about that simple act – and instantly we all recognized the stranger in our midst! It was JESUS! He was in our home – alive – sitting at our table! Jesus!

Did we see the nail-pierced hands – or did we see in our minds eye a flashback to similar provisions for 5000 which stirred us to awareness? I cannot say. I only know for certain it was Him! And the next instant, He was gone – vanished from our sight!

Well, Cleopas and Benjamin hit the road running – running back the 7 miles to Jerusalem. Forgotten the discouragement, the doubts, and the fears! Forgotten the tiredness and confusion. Only one thing mattered – Jesus is ALIVE!!! They must tell everyone! He had walked with them by the way – He had talked to them of the Scriptures – and He had met us right in our own home – and then vanished!

But before He left so quickly, as He was breaking that bread, I saw again that look of love….and as He looked at me, this time I knew He was saying – "I did this for you…..and because I live, you shall live also – really live!"

He's ALIVE – Jesus is ALIVE – forevermore! Hallelujah!

OLD AND NEW TESTAMENT
MONOLOGUES COMBINED

SECTION V – A FAMILY
DEVOTIONAL WALK

A Family Devotional Walk

*T*his walk was written and designed for an outdoor setting, with 5 separate scenes. All of the characters were in Biblical costumes, and various props were used to enhance the setting. In every case, only the narrator spoke, so that others in the scene remained stationary during the presentation.

Of course, there is no reason why this could not be adapted to an indoor setting – such as multiple rooms in a church or other facility.

We had a group of several hundred people which we separated into 5 smaller groups for the walk. Each group had a leader to take them to each scene, and each group started with a different scene, and rotated until they had visited them all. Each group leader was also in Biblical costume, and led the groups in singing the chorus "He is Able" (Rory Noland/Greg Ferguson) as they walked to each scene.

Chapter 15

Elisha and the Widow's Oil

Text: II Kings 4: 1-7
Location: A Small Bible-Time Home (Interior)
Characters: Elisha, Widow, Two Sons,
Narrator (A Creditor)

(The Creditor greets everyone, shaking his head, and clutching a fist full of money)

Good morning – good morning! I am Benjamin Bar Ahab – a coppersmith by trade – have my own small shop down in the marketplace.

Pardon me if I seem a bit puzzled. I'm still trying to figure out what happened here....strangest thing I have ever seen! Why, just a few days ago, that widow woman over there, was as poor as poor could be. She didn't have one shekel to rub against another one! As a matter of fact, some of the other merchants and I were preparing to take her two sons as slaves. They were to be our servants for 7 years – work for us, and help pay off all the family debts.

I hated to do it. I've got sons of my own – and her husband was a good man – a prophet himself – from our school of prophecy, here in Gilgal. He was faithful – as good a provider as he could be, for a prophet. Sure, I felt sorry for his wife and sons – but, hey! Business is business – and I have to look out for myself, too!

Well, I guess she was not about to give up those boys of hers – so she appealed to the prophet Elisha. The way I heard it, he asked her what she had in the house that was of any value. Seems all she had to her name was a small pitcher of olive oil – on the mantelpiece over there.

Elisha told her to gather all the empty jars she could find – to go from house to house all over town. I guess she and the lads covered every street, bringing back empty vases, jars, pitchers – whatever people would give them. I know they came to our house, and my wife gave them a couple of stone water pots we weren't using....

When they collected all they could find, they went inside here, and shut the door. No one else actually saw what happened next. But Rueben, the eldest son, told me it was a MIRACLE – right before their eyes!

Elisha told the widow to start pouring out the olive oil from her little pitcher – into all those jars they had collected. Look, I find it hard to believe myself – but Ruben told me that EVERY CONTAINER in their house was filled to the brim! Jars of oil everywhere! And when they ran out of jars, the oil stopped flowing!

I wish I could have seen it! It must have been true- because after that, Elisha told them to sell the oil, and pay off all their debts. That's how I got my money – and Ruben says they have enough left over to start a small business venture of their own, and keep the family together!

Oh, I've never been much of a believer myself – but I have to admire the faith of that little woman. She told me, if she would have had more empty jars, there would have been more oil! She said, "The way to increase what we have, is to give it away!" She trusted God enough to give up the very last drop of her only possession. She's been going around telling everyone that when she came to the end of herself – she came to the beginning of God!

Who knows? This all might just make a believer out of me, too! I can't deny this fist full of money from a penniless widow – and I can't deny that there is obviously a God in Israel Who is MORE THAN ABLE to meet the MATERIAL needs of a family who trusts in Him!

Chapter 16

The Healing of Naaman

Text: II Kings 5: 1-14

Location: A Syrian Home – suitable for the Capt. Of the King's Army!

Characters: Naaman, Mrs. Naaman, Servant Girl, Narrator (A Male servant who had accompanied Naaman to Israel)

(Male servant of Naaman's greets everyone)

*H*ello friends – come in, come in! My name is Joel, and I am a servant to Naaman over there.

You will have to forgive me if I seem a bit tired. We just returned from a long trip into Israel. I have had more than my share of chariot driving lately, I can tell you! Ah, but it was worth every mile! See that smile on my master's face? He has a lot to be happy about NOW......but he sure did not look that way a few days ago!

You see, Naaman is a pretty big guy around here – Captain of the Army of the King of Syria, to be exact. Sort of the "prime minister" of the state. At his word, troops come and go – military strategy is planned and carried out. He's a strong man, honorable, smart – and he likes to win! But Naaman had one BIG problem – he had leprosy. That's a dread disease that sort of eats holes in your skin – and nobody wants to touch you. Most people who get it, have to leave their homes, families and work – and live secluded lives, until the disease brings about their death. Yes, Naaman was as great as he could be, and yet, the lowliest slave in Syria would not change places with him!

Naaman kept up his work, but he knew it would not last forever, and he was worried about his future. And the KING was worried, too.

That's why everyone was happy when their servant girl spoke up. That's her over there (gesture). She was brought back captive from Israel, to wait on Naaman's wife. They love her as their own daughter, though, and I believe that she loves them too. She told Naaman's wife one day that she wished her master could get together with the prophet Elisha over in Samaria. "He could heal him of his leprosy" she declared with confidence.

Well, naturally, Mrs. Naaman told Naaman, Naaman told the King and the next thing I know,

we've got a whole caravan of horses and char-
iots heading out for Israel. The boss took plenty
of gold, silver and fine clothing as gifts for his
healing. He also took a letter to the King of Israel
– from the King of Syria. We were an impressive
parade – I must say!

Our first stop in Israel was to deliver the
King's letter. It basically said – "This is my servant Naaman. He has leprosy, and I need you to
heal him." Signed – the King of Syria.

Well, the King of Israel was NOT a happy man,
when he read that letter. As a matter of fact, he
tore his royal robes as a sign of his frustration.
He thought the other King was asking him to
play god, and do the impossible. He was sure the
Syrian King was trying to pick a fight with him!

So – we didn't go anywhere for a few days,
until Elisha heard about the King's temper tan-
trum and sent a message which said – "Have the
man come to me – and he will know there is a
prophet in Israel."

Now that's more like it! Naaman was going
to get a personal audience with the prophet – or
perhaps to Naaman's thinking, the prophet was
going to have a personal audience with him!

Actually, it didn't happen either way, because
when we arrived at Elisha's place – all primed and
polished – he didn't even come out to meet us!
Instead, he sent his servant with a message – "Go,

wash yourself seven times in the Jordan, and your flesh will be restored and you will be cleansed."

Well – you thought the King of Israel was mad – Naaman was FURIOUS!

First of all – he thought Elisha would come out, make a big fuss over him – publically call on God, name him in prayer – wave his hands around a few times and – "ta-dum" – NO MORE LEPROSY!

Secondly, Elisha didn't show any honor to Syria, by ordering him to wash in the muddy Jordan, instead of the crystal clear rivers of Damascus.

Naaman grumbled and pouted – stomping off like a spoiled child, muttering about his displeasure – actually ready to go back home without even TRYING what Elisha had commanded!

We let him rant and rave for a while – and then the other servants and I approached him.

("Master,") we said, "if the prophet had asked you to do some great thing – would you not have done it? How much more then when he tells you wash and be cleansed!" I mean, it seemed reasonable to us – the promise was clear – "You WILL be clean" – and the method was plain – "Go wash in the Jordan." He had nothing to lose......but his leprosy!

So, he finally agreed to make the 25 mile trip to the Jordan. I must admit, it was rather humbling to see this mighty Syrian leader wading into that muddy river.....but we were all cheering for him – shouting and counting on the shore.

" 1 – 2 – 3 – that's it, boss! 4 – 5 –don't quit now Master! -6 -7 times. "No one spoke a word as we waited for our master to emerge from the water after the count of seven. One look at his face told the story – he began to shout and laugh at the same time....."I'm clean – I'm clean....I'm healed – I'm HEALED!" THERE WAS DANCING ON THE SHORE, TOO – I CAN TELL YOU!

Naaman hasn't stopped smiling – and the ride home was a jubilant one, all right!

Thank God for the Israelite servant-girl. Strange thing – you know, Elisha had never healed a leper before.....how did she KNOW, without any doubt, that he would do it for Naaman?

I guess that is FAITH – and that little girl showed everyone the God Who is MORE THAN ABLE to meet the PHYSICAL needs of a family who trusts in Him!

Chapter 17

The Raising of Lazarus

Text: John 11: 1-44

Location: Outside a Tomb in Bethany

Characters: Mary, Martha, Lazarus – Narrator (A Neighbor)

Suggested props: (in addition to costumes) a tomb, with rolled away "stone" – some gauze, or strips of cloth still semi-bound around Lazarus

(Neighbor speaks)

*O*h, yes, I've seen Jesus come and go many times from their little home in Bethany. My name is Abigail – and I've been their neighbor across the way for a good many years. Jesus seemed to find it restful and secure with them

– they were all his friends – Mary, Martha and Lazarus.

I was surprised, then, that Jesus did not come right away when He got the message that Lazarus was sick. Why, Bethany is less than 2 miles from Jerusalem!

I can tell you, Martha was stunned! Bewildered. She thought surely Jesus would come to heal Lazarus – but He didn't. Then, she thought surely He would be there for the funeral – but He wasn't! By the time He did make it, Lazarus was four days in the grave, and Martha felt their friend had let them down!

She had often confided in me before Lazarus died. She was expecting Jesus to come! After all, hadn't He healed others? The lame? The blind? The leper? And none of those people were as close to Jesus as Lazarus was – they were like blood brothers! Why? Why didn't He come?

The one person, who could have done some-thing to change the situation, didn't – and Martha wanted an explanation! So when she heard He was nearing their home, she marched determinedly out to meet Him.

"Lord, if you had been here," she accused, "my brother would not have died."

'Jesus met Martha on the ragged edge of mourning and loss. He spoke not of death, but of life!

"I am the resurrection and the Life." Jesus told her – "He who believes in me will live, even though he dies."

Then Jesus asked Martha to go and get Mary. He apparently wanted a private word with her, too. Mary came – her eyes blurred with tears, her heart crushed, her emotions in turmoil, as she fell in a heap at His feet, pouring out her pain.

"Lord, if you had been here," she blurted out, "my brother would not have died."

They had so counted on Him, believed in Him. Their grief was doubled by the absence of this friend who could have made a difference!

Mary was followed by many of the other mourners – who came, thinking she had gone to the tomb to weep.

Jesus was deeply troubled – like He was wrestling with some sort of force that no one else could see.

He asked to be taken to the grave. On His way there, walking along the road with the others – Jesus wept....openly, unashamedly. It was a strange, yet beautiful co-mingling of divinity and humanity in that one tender moment.

As Mary and Martha saw and felt His obvious compassion – their hurt and pain began to disappear. Just His very presence still made a difference!

Arriving at the tomb, Jesus requested that the stone be rolled back from the door. Everyone took a few steps backward as Martha spoke all our thoughts.

"But Lord, by this time there is a bad odor, for he has been there four days!"

"Did I not tell you," He said, " that if you believe, you would see the glory of God?"

So – the stone was rolled back. A deafening hush came over the wailing crowd, as Jesus lifted His voice in prayer.

It was a simple prayer of thanksgiving to God, ending with a brief request that people would believe in God because of what was about to happen.

With that, Jesus shouted out the command – "Lazarus – COME FORTH!"

No one dared even breathe, as we strained our ears to hear a stir – a rustle.....and suddenly, THERE HE WAS IN THE DOORWAY – LAZARUS – still bound about with the grave clothes! Jesus commanded the people to loose him, and let him go.

It was an incredible moment of reunion and joy, mingled with shock and disbelief! Wailing turned to laughter – dismay gave way to a glorious hope! Many people ran back to the city to spread the word about Jesus! What a thrill it was for me to be an eye-witness to all these happenings!

But you know, I really believe that even if Lazarus had not been raised to life again – Mary and Martha would still have been helped, cheered, and comforted by Jesus' very presence with them. They discovered that God is MORE THAN ABLE to meet the EMOTIONAL needs of a family who trusts in Him!

Chapter 18

Midnight Praises

Text: Acts 16: 16-34

Location: The Jailer's Home

Characters: Paul, Silas, Jailer and Family,

Narrator: Another Prison Guard

(The Prison Guard speaks)

*G*reetings! Welcome to the home of Timothy, better known as – the Philippian Jailer. My name is Marcus – and I too, am a prison guard.

I was working the "grave yard" shift last night, when Paul and Silas were brought in. They were a MESS – all bruised and bleeding.....having been beaten with rods, and dragged over the cobble stone streets.

I overheard the authorities tell Timothy here that these prisoners were to be guarded with his life – and if anything happened to them......well, he'd better be prepared to pay the consequences!

So, Timothy put them in the inner holding cell – with chains on their wrists, and their feet in stocks. They weren't going anywhere – for a long time!

I figured these two must be violent, dangerous criminals – so I asked Timothy what horrible deed they had done to deserve this punishment. Turns out, there was a lot of confusion about the case, but it seems that they were simply teaching and preaching in the name of Christ! A young slave girl from the city began following them everywhere. She was possessed by an evil spirit, and brought her masters much money by her fortune-telling powers. While Paul and the others with him were trying to tell people about Christ, this girl kept interrupting and shouting – "These men are the servants of the highest God, who are telling you the way to be saved!"

Though what she was saying was true, the gospel they were trying to proclaim would certainly be questioned by an association with a demon-possessed slave-girl.

She kept doing this to them for many days – until Paul became greatly annoyed. He turned and spoke to the spirit within her – "In the name of Jesus Christ, I command you to come out of her!".....and he came out immediately!

Well, of course, when her masters found out about what had happened – they were outraged! Obviously, the powers within this girl that had been lining their greedy pockets with money

– was gone. She was no good to them anymore. So, they angrily seized Paul and Silas, and dragged them into the Marketplace. They falsely accused them of troubling the city – and teaching customs which were not right for the Romans to observe. The townspeople got caught up in the fervor of anger and hostility – and became a blood-thirsty mob! The authorities publicly stripped Paul and Silas, and commanded that they be beaten with rods and imprisoned.

That's when I met them. This all sounded so unfair, and they seemed like gentle and harm-less men to me – men who had been misjudged and mistreated. But, that was not ours to deter-mine – our job was to see that they didn't escape, whether we agreed with the charges or not!

They were secure, all right – so Timothy and I settled down for the night. Along about midnight, we were awakened by a strange series of events. First, there was singing! That's right – from the inner dark cave of a cell – Paul and Silas were actually singing – and praising God! I couldn't believe it! They HAD to feel miserable and be in terrible pain and discomfort. But they put all of that aside to sing! The other prisoners heard it, too – but before any of us really had time to react or respond – there came a much louder, and awful sound – an EARTHQUAKE!

The entire prison shook – even the very foun-dations! The prison doors were opened – and

everyone's chains fell off! It all happened so fast.....
and it was so dark, we couldn't see a thing! But
as soon as Timothy realized the doors were all
opened – he took out his sword, and was going to
kill himself! He knew he would have to pay with
his life anyhow, if those prisoners had escaped –
so, he might as well get it over with! I was going
to try to stop him myself – when I heard Paul's
voice calling out – "Don't harm yourself – we are
all here!" Can you believe it? Not one prisoner had
even TRIED to leave!

Timothy called for a light – so I brought him
a torch, and he called Paul and Silas out before
him. Trembling, he fell on his knees and said,
"Sirs, what must I do to be saved?" I found myself
kneeling, too – along with others.

Their answer was quite simple – "Believe
in the Lord Jesus Christ, and you will be saved
– you and your household!" How could we NOT
believe, after all we had witnessed that night! The
God of Paul and Silas had certainly become very
real to us!

Well, I secured the rest of the prisoners – and
Timothy took Paul and Silas home with him!

They never did get to bed last night. Timothy
and his wife made them feel at home, dressed their
wounds, and then – Timothy couldn't wait until
morning – he and everyone in his family received
Christ – right there in his home! Afterward, he had
food set out for a festive meal – it was a night to

remember! I came over as soon as I could, when my relief came, to join in the celebration! Praise God! What an unforgettable night!

Oh, I tell you, I have seen that God is MORE THAN ABLE to meet the SPIRITUAL needs of a family who trusts in Him!

Chapter 19

A Miracle in Cana

Text: John 2: 1-11

Location: Outdoor Pavilion
Characters: Bride, Groom, Parents/Family
Narrator: Father of the Bride
(The Father of the Bride speaks)

*A*h! Welcome! We've been expecting you. Welcome to the celebration – our daughter's marriage feast!

Ah! So much joy and happiness! I am glad you came – I want EVERYONE to share in the miracle!

Yes, I DID say MIRACLE! I, Jacob Ben Ahbed, and all my guests here – witnessed a simple, yet most wonderful miracle!

But, let me start at the beginning. You see, a wedding in the day of Christ is a long, extravagant affair! This wedding began with a ceremony at the synagogue, at sundown. People then left the synagogue, and began parading through the city, winding their way up and down the streets of town. The couple was led past many homes, so everyone could see them and wish them well.

After the processional, they have come home – to a PARTY!

How the common people look forward to such an event! For a few days and hours they can share a common joy with friends, lay aside their work load and meager lifestyle and celebrate! The plates are filled and refilled with good food – and the cups are raised and filled to the brim again and again! It is my pleasure and responsibility as the host, to make sure we never run out of food or wine! Hospitality here is my sacred duty – and a serious one at that!

To run out of wine is a social embarrassment, to say the least. Wine is not present for drunkenness, but rather for the statement it makes that this is a very special occasion, and that each guest is equally special!

Well, to my horror and dismay, the unthinkable happened – the wine ran out! Surely we had arranged for enough! How could we have miscalculated? Where could I go at this late hour to replenish the supply?

Now Jesus of Nazareth was here – He and his mother, and a few of His followers. Mary sensed right away our awkward situation, and went to Jesus on our behalf.

"They have no more wine." She told Him plainly. Since the day of His birth, Mary has been waiting expectantly – waiting to see Jesus display the wondrous powers she believes in her heart that He possesses. Was this the right moment? After all – there was a need – no one could deny that – surely He could do SOMETHING!

Jesus hesitated, I understand. I was too busy pacing back and forth, wringing my hands to notice. But the servants told me later that Mary slipped quietly to them and said, "Do whatever He tells you!" Even though it seemed Jesus had turned aside from her plea, she still believed He would do the right thing!

Perhaps Jesus hesitated, knowing that once He crossed this threshold, and did this miracle, His obscurity would be forever gone. The solace and seclusion of the carpenter shop would be a closed chapter of His life, as word about this miracle spread from town to town. His life would be an open book – His time calculated. I don't know, but my servants said, as Jesus pensively held a wine goblet in His hands – He had a faraway look in His eyes – as if the object represented something ominous to Him.

As He reflected on all of that – so He reflected on our needs. The people here – so oppressed and so burdened.....so many barely eking out an existence – so in need of a little joyful merrymaking in their lives. And we, the parents of the bride and groom – so weary with all our festal preparations – so encumbered to make possible this wedding. And, the bride and groom themselves – this social, family embarrassment would be no way to start a marriage, or a new life together in the community. The newlyweds needed help – and His heart was moved with compassion for them!

Jesus moved to tell the servants to fill up those water pots over there – those water pots used for ceremonial washings – AND to serve the head table from them!

Somewhere between the filling and the pouring, that water blushed to red and delighted the taste buds of every guest more than any previous wine we had served! The water – became the wine – by the whispered will of Jesus!

It happened right here –in this poor, obscure village of Cana! No announcement – no hocuspocus – no showmanship. Just God quietly seeing and understanding our human needs – and meeting us at the point of our need!

Mary told us all along that He was God's Son. I doubted before – but I believe it NOW!

This miracle told me that what matters to me, matters to God! I knew God cared about the big things like – sin, disease, death and disaster....but a shortage of wine at a wedding? I mean, He's got the sun, moon and stars of the galaxies to keep in their places – monarchs to protect – prayers to answer. After all, He's the Creator – the Ruler of this universe!

Still, it was obvious – what concerned me, concerned Him. If it touches the child, it moves the Father!

Ah, we learned a GREAT truth today – that our God is MORE THAN ABLE – yes, and even longs- to meet ANY need of a family who trusts in Him!

SECTION VI- SISTERS ACROSS THE CENTURIES

The following 10 monologues were originally written especially for a women's weekend event entitled "Precious in His Sight"

The concept is that a modern woman speaks about a problem or concern she is facing, and the Biblical woman responds from her own life experience in a similar situation.

These could be performed in one setting, or each chapter could be performed separately for 5 consecutive weeks as a part of worship, or a Bible study discussion. They could also simply be used individually, to go along with a particular theme. The possibilities are endless! Enjoy!

Chapter 20A:

Modern Woman – The Diagnosis

I've just been diagnosed with advanced, inoperable cancer!

More rounds of doctors, hospitals – treatments – medications – and still no real hope. Already I feel alone. People have tired of my recital of complaints. No one wants to hear about it anymore – they don't even ask. Now, they'll be afraid to touch me – embrace me – care for me. It's been this way for years with me. I've spent all my money on doctors, and still they couldn't pin point the problem – until now. And now, it's too late!

I feel some relief, strangely. At least I know now the enemy I'm fighting. But the prospects are dark – hope is diminished, the future to be dreaded – death is almost certain.

I'm afraid. It's not just that I don't want to leave my family and what few friends I have here – but it's not knowing what comes after that – what lies beyond? I don't feel ready for that!

And where is God in all of this? If He loves me so much – why would He let this happen to me – why do I have to suffer like this?

I want Him to touch me....or I want to touch Him.....but how can I get to Him through all of this pain, this doubt, this haunting fear and uncertainty?

I feel jostled about in the crowd – void of purpose.....does He care? Does He know I'm here – reaching out to Him?

Chapter 20B:

Response: The Woman with the Issue of Blood

Text: Matthew 9: 18-22; Mark 5: 21-34; Luke 8: 40 -48

*Y*es, my sister, He knows you are reaching out to Him....and if you can but touch the hem of His garment – you will experience healing, wholeness and health! Oh, it may not be an immediate cure for your disease – but still, you can be made perfectly whole....

Let me tell you my story.....

For 12 long years, I had a flow of blood – a uterine hemorrhage, to be exact. I was tired, weak from constant blood loss, frail and anemic. I had gone from physician to physician – faithfully following their orders and trying all sorts of folk remedies – even those that sounded ridiculous and absurd.

Nothing happened. The only thing that stopped was my flow of money – it had all been pressed into the palms of those physicians – and I was getting worse by the day. Now, not only was I sick, I was poor.

Perhaps the most excruciating pain of all – was that of loneliness and separation. You see, because of the nature of my ailment, I was "ceremonially unclean." I could not worship at the temple, could not mingle with the people, could not touch or be touched. I had to continually declare verbally that the discharge was still happening. My dreams of marriage – family – fulfillment – lay shattered around me, as I trudged the back alleyways of town scrounging for a scrap of hope – a morsel of promise!

The doctors had finally confessed that I was beyond hope. They knew I had no more money to spend. Money talks, they say, and I had nothing more to say – and as a result, they had nothing more to offer

But there was one physician I had never tried. A Galilean carpenter who was routing demons, restoring lepers, and releasing the paralyzed. It had been noised about that that Jesus had actually touched the leper when He healed him!

Surely – if He touched a leper – He would touch me – or maybe I did not even need Him to touch me – if I could touch Him.....that's it, I thought! It was worth a try! If His garment would just brush my fingertips – I believed I could be healed!

He was coming to town – crowds were already gathering – how could I get past them all? Everyone knew me – everyone avoided me. I could literally be thrown out of the city gate if I were caught inside. Still, hope grew within me – a strength I had not felt in years began to pulsate through my body as I carried out my plans.

I covered my head and face – crawled on my hands and knees through the throng. I slithered on my stomach at times, past the sandaled feet – then, at just the right moment – I reached out and touched just the tassel of His prayer shawl - that's all it took!

The very moment His robe brushed my hand – I felt His healing! The flowing blood stopped, new health and vitality came to my body. I felt stronger, younger – I felt whole again!

Suddenly, Jesus stopped in His tracks. "Who touched me?" He asked. His followers look puzzled. People were pressed in against Him – countless individuals had touched Him. Jesus persisted, "Someone touched me; "He said, "I know that power has gone out from me."

Trembling, I pushed through the people and fell down before Him. I told Him my whole story and why I had touched Him.

"Daughter," He said gently – "your faith has healed you. Go in peace."

Truly, the most precious word He spoke was to call me "daughter" – for in that word He declared my worth to all who heard! I was His child – no longer an unclean outcast.

The healing was secondary. I am deeply grateful, of course, to be rid of the plague and the pain – but to belong to Him is the best part of all. To be His daughter – His child – His own - that is what makes life worthwhile!

And sister – even if there is not physical healing for you – and who can know the mind of God – He can lift you up – heal your spirit and soul – and make you whole and complete in Him! That is, after all, the ultimate healing! Reach out in faith sister – reach out! You are precious to Him!

Chapter 21A:

Modern Woman – The New Widow

God took my husband from me – suddenly – unexpectedly – heart attack. I had no time to prepare myself, or my sons for this loss.

We were never rich – but when he lived, we were at least comfortable. Now we are poor. All the money is gone, and still the bills aren't all paid. My sons are too young to work, and I cannot work and leave them in someone else's care all day. I don't have any training or skills – I just wanted to be a mother!

I am afraid the authorities are going to take my children from me because I can't provide for them. I lay awake at night worrying about how I'm going to get out of this mess!

The cupboards are bare – the food is gone, and my sons are crying in hunger!

My husband was a good man – he trusted God to take care of him and us. I miss him so much! I am trying to trust, too – but staring at empty cupboards and a stack of unpaid bills is not helping. If I'm so precious to God – why doesn't He come down here and do something?

Chapter 21B:

Response:
The Widow and her Cruse of Oil

Text: II Kings 4: 1-7

*Y*our story is my story, sister. We are twins
– born centuries apart – our lives and our
circumstances divinely intertwined.

I, too, was a widow – with two young sons. My
husband was one of the "sons of the prophets" – a
student-follower of the prophets Elijah and Elisha.

He died suddenly, leaving us with a godly heritage, but no provision for our future needs. I found
myself with no husband, no income, no food, and
no prospects. What little money I had was quickly
gone – and word was spreading that if I could not
pay my debts, the creditors would come to take my
young sons as slaves. This practice was allowed
by Mosaic Law, but the law was being abused and

misused! My sons were so young – and also, how could I bear to lose them when I had already suffered the loss of their father – my dear husband?

I wanted to help myself – but I did not know where to turn. As I was thinking on this, and earnestly seeking God, I felt led to go to the man of God himself – Elisha. After all, my husband had been one of his devoted followers – and they were pledged to take care of their own!

I was a bit fearful – but I had no other choice – I had to ask for help. Just sharing with Elisha seemed to ease my burden – I sensed somehow the answer was on the way!

Elisha asked me what I had in the house – and I pointed to this small jar of olive oil on the mantel.

"Go all around and ask all your neighbors for empty jars", Elisha told me, Don't ask for just a few!"

It seemed like a strange request – but I was desperate for help and I trusted the man of God. My sons helped me – gladly. We went up and down all the streets asking for vessels – jars and pots from everyone we met.

At first, I was afraid – but the people were kind, and seemed glad to do anything to help us. No one refused us or turned us away – and by the end of the day, our small house was filled with empty jars and containers of every size and shape!

Elisha instructed me to take my two sons with me into the room with all the empty vessels – to shut the door behind us – and then to take that small cruse of oil from the mantel, and begin to fill up all those containers we had collected from neighbors and friends!

I could not believe what happened next! From that small jar of oil near the fireplace, came enough oil to fill EVERY jar and vessel we had borrowed! It was absolutely amazing – it kept pouring and pouring and pouring – and when we had filled every container to the brim, the oil stopped! If there had been more vessels, there would have been more oil, I know! My two sons were speechless, and I was weeping for joy!

When I told Elisha that all the jars were full, he said – "Go, sell the oil and pay your debts. You and your sons can live on what is left." And it has been just as he said.

I had to bring EMPTY vessels to be filled. I learned that day that emptiness can be a wonderful gift! I had to first admit that I had a need – I was empty – I had nothing! I learned that my "nothing" given in faith became "abundance" in the hands of God!

I needed to "shut the door" to be alone with God to experience the miracle. This was a private miracle of grace and mercy for me and my sons. Not even Elisha was in that room with us – just my sons, me, all those empty jars – and GOD – God in His infinite power and provision! My own faith was greatly strengthened – and the boys will never forget it! They will no doubt still be telling it to their children's children!

Start with what you have, my sister – and give that back to God. He will use what you give Him to help answer your prayers. If you are not experiencing God's presence and provision – could it be that you are not empty enough? Could you still be distracted and dependent on yourself?

He provided more than enough for me – and I know He can do the same for you! You are precious to Him! He WILL take care of you! He is able – MORE than able!

Chapter 22A:

Modern Woman – The Lost Son

*D*oesn't God understand my pain?

For years, my husband and I were childless. It seemed that we would never be blessed with a family – and that we would have to accept that fact. Just when we were about to give up all hope – the great news came that I was pregnant! We were thrilled!

We had many pleasures in our life together – but this would be the crowning joy!

Before many months passed, we learned our child was a boy. That made it even greater – for now, the family name would be carried on for generations to come.

He was born in the spring of the year – an absolutely perfect baby boy! When I held him, and looked into his face for the first time – I thought surely I must be dreaming! I felt so unworthy. But I also felt a tremendous responsibility.

He was only two weeks old the first time we took him to church. We wanted him to grow up knowing and loving the people who had loved and prayed for him long before he was even born.

How he loved life! He enjoyed our church – sang in the "Angel" choir – took part in the pageants and plays – became active in the youth fellowship when he was a teen – and later, was given the privilege of teaching the Junior Boys Sunday School Class.

We were so proud of him! He had grown to be a fine young man – handsome, confident, and honest.

Too honest, I guess – because one night, he sat down with us in our living room, and told us he was leaving home. He said he could no longer put up a façade. His lifestyle and desires were much different from ours, he said, and he was moving out! He had friends, and a place to go. It was too confining for him to co-exist with us!

That's when the pain began. He rarely phones – we never see him. His choices have cast a shadow of shame across our family name – and have pierced us through to our very souls!

It's as if he died. But I know he is out there somewhere! Would to God he had never been born! It would have been easier to remain childless than to have him in our hearts as we do – and see him walk away from the principles and ideals in which we believe!

Sometimes I want to pour out my pain to all my friends at church – and other times, I am so ashamed that I cannot bear to speak of it! I cry out my anger and frustration to God.

How can I keep hoping? How can I know God cares about this awful pain?

Chapter 22B:

Response:
The Shunemmite Woman

Text: II Kings 4: 8-37

*O*h, do not despair, my sister. Never give up hope. Never stop trusting God to hear and answer your prayers!

I think I know how you feel – for I, too, lost a son – an only child.

My husband and I lived in the village of Shunem, a village on the edge of the rich grain field of Esdraelon – at the base of Mt. Carmel.

We lived comfortably, and were well known and established among our people.

The prophet Elisha often passed through our village – right past our home. We heard about his preaching and miracles, and perceived him to be a holy man of God.

One day, we invited him inside for some rest and a bit of food. We enjoyed his company – and he ours, so much that he began to come by quite often. It seemed we had become a refuge for him, and his servant Gehazi. In fact, we even decided to add a room to our house – just for him! It had an outside entrance, so that he could go and come at will. This "prophet's chamber" was simply furnished – a bed, a table, a stool, and a lampstand. But, it seemed to become a very sacred place to Elisha.

During one of his visits with us, he called me to him and asked what he could do for me, in return for all that we had done for him. Could he put in a good word for us to the King? Or to the Captain of the Host? I assured him I was quite content among my own people. There was nothing I needed! He called me back to his room later, and told me that within a year, I would have a child – and it would be a son!

I could not believe what he was saying – surely, I must not even hope that this could be. My husband was much older than I, and we had long ago accepted the fact that we would never have a child. Still, something within me made me trust Elisha's words!

It came to pass, just as Elisha had said. By the next spring, our son was born – and my heart was overflowing with joy! Truly, this child had come through the blessing of the man of God – and he must be a special child indeed!

How we delighted in watching him grow. Now the prophet often came just to play with our son, and to hold him on his knee. In no time, it seemed, our little boy was walking and talking – the months and years went by swiftly!

It was harvest time one year, and our son begged his father to let him go into the fields with him. We thought it would be all right – there were many workers to keep watch over him.

But the sun was beating down that day – and there were so many working in the fields that no one noticed that our son did not retreat to the shade, or go for a cool drink by the well. He kept working in the heat of the sun. Suddenly, he ran to his father – "My head, my head!" he cried. That's when one of the servants brought him to me. I held him on my lap and rocked and comforted him – but all to no avail. At noonday – he died. He died in my arms!

How my heart broke in that moment – but I knew what I had to do – and there was no time to waste!

I took my little boy's lifeless body, and laid him on the bed in the prophet's chamber – and shut the door. Then, I went to the field, and asked my husband for a servant and a donkey that I might go to Mt. Carmel to see that man of God, Elisha. My husband wondered why I was going that day, since it was not the Sabbath, or a holy day. I told him not to be concerned – that all was well!

The servant and I left for Mt. Carmel. I told him to go straight ahead, and not to go slow on my account – unless I told him to slow down.

We spared no time in traveling those 15 miles – and while we were yet a great way off, Gehazi came to meet us, inquiring if all was well.

"Everything is all right," I said, and kept on going – I had to see the man of God!

Suddenly, when I saw Elisha, I could contain my grief no longer, and I fell at his feet. Gehazi tried to push me away, but Elisha saw my deep despair, and waited for me to pour out my soul to him.

"Did I ask you for a son, my lord?" I said. "Didn't I tell you, 'Don't raise my hopes'?"

Elisha seemed to know immediately that my son had died. He sent Gehazi to my house with his staff, and told him to lay it on the child's face.

"As surely as the Lord lives and as you live, I will not leave you," I told Elisha. I knew only he could be used by God – if there was to be a miracle at all!

So we went together toward my home in Shunem. As we were going, Gehazi met us with news that the child had not awakened.

Presently, Elisha came into his chamber – and saw the child lying on his bed. He shut the door.

I retreated to my own room to pray. I am not sure what happened in that chamber. I heard Elisha pacing back and forth, back and forth – and then it would become quiet. He told me later how he laid his own body on my son's – and thus prayed to God for a miracle!

Then I heard a strange, yet wonderful sound. I heard my son sneezing! Seven times he sneezed – and then Elisha said he opened his eyes!

Gehazi called me to come up. I ran up the steps! "Take your son!" Elisha said, smiling at me!

Oh, I fell at his feet – bowed down to the ground in gratitude and praise to our God! Then I picked up my son, and held him tightly in my arms. I hurried out to show him alive to my husband – and to tell my story to all who would listen!

Oh, my sister – I never gave up hope that God would restore my son. In the midst of my pain and sorrow, I actually praised Him! "Everything is all right," I said – "Everything is all right" – and God rewarded my faith!

It is hard for you to believe that your son could ever be restored. I know – I feel your pain. But so does our God! He cares – He understands! You are precious to Him! Give your son into God's keeping, and say within yourself – and yes, even to those who ask you – "All is well.....hallelujah, all is well!"

Chapter 23A:

Modern Woman –
The Ashamed Woman

*S*ometimes I look at my reflection in the mirror and wonder who that woman is. I've lived over half my life, but what have I done? What good have I accomplished? The light seems gone from my eyes – the laughter lines replaced with furrowed brow and darkened circles. And no wonder. I've nothing to be proud of – only shame in my past and my present. I've botched up my life. It's a well-known fact.

I've indulged myself in one relationship after another. So many men – I've lost count. I've been married a few times – but mostly had live-in lovers and one night stands.

Oh, I have a reputation, all right – a sordid one!

I changed shifts at work – my request – because no one would sit at the same table with me at lunch, or work alongside of me in the office.

People avoided me like the plague. They would whisper about me when I entered the room. I have no friends – and I can't blame them – I don't think very highly of myself either. People think I like the kind of life I lead – but to be honest, I'm miserable. I'm sick of it.

I wish there was a way out – a way I could be different – better. But, I've been this way so long I can't seem to find my way out. Besides, no one else would ever believe in me, or hope with me that I could change.

It started a long time ago with me. I was abused in the lowest kind of way as a child. I guess I grew up believing that was the only way to give and receive love. But I don't love myself – so how can I love anyone else? I don't think I know the meaning of the word.

Yesterday, near the water cooler at work, I found a pamphlet. I think the new guy that just started working at the office last month left it there. Anyhow, the pamphlet was about Jesus – His love – His forgiveness – a chance to start life over again.

Do you think there's any truth to what is written in that pamphlet?

Could Jesus really love me?

Could He forgive all my past shame and sin?

If I thought there was even a chance...........

Chapter 23B:

Response – The Samaritan Woman

Text: John 4: 1 -42

$\mathscr{B}$elieve me, my sister, there is more than a chance – there is assurance that Jesus will receive and forgive you!

I know, because He did it for me – and our stories are not that different, even though we belong to different centuries.

I came to the well at Sychar every day at noon to draw water. I chose midday to come because no one else ever came at that time. It gave me time to be alone, and also kept me isolated from the stares and whispered condemnation of the other women who came in the morning and evening.

That day was like any other, except that as I made my way to the well, I felt the weight of more than the water pot on my shoulder. I felt the ugly, terrible weight of my wasted life.

I was <u>the</u> woman of Samaria. Everyone knew my past – and my ongoing lifestyle. A string of broken marriages – and the man I was with at the time was not my husband.

On my way to the well that day, I was thinking of a beautiful young girl I once knew – full of life, promise and possibilities. Carefree. Happy. Alive!

Broken hearts, shattered dreams and bad choices had pushed that innocent girl so far down, down deep inside of me, that I knew in my heart she could never be restored. I would have to live out the rest of my days as hollow and empty as the water pot I was carrying.

When I wearily rounded the last bend in the dusty road – I saw him there by the well. A stranger. A man. A Jew.

What was He doing there? I didn't want to talk to anyone – see anyone. I just wanted to be left alone!

As I approached, He spoke to me – "Will you give me a drink?"

I was suspicious – guarded. "You are a Jew and I am a Samaritan woman. How can you ask me for a drink?" I asked. ("For the Jews do not associate with Samaritans.") Besides, it was not lawful for a man to even speak to a woman in public.

"If you knew the gift of God – and Who it is that asks you for a drink," He said, "you would have asked him and he would have given you living water."

Sir," I said to Him – "you have nothing to draw with and the well is deep!" Did He think He was greater than our fathers who dug the well, and passed it on to us?

"Everyone who drinks this water will be thirsty again, but whoever drinks the water I give them will never thirst. Indeed, the water I give them will become in them a spring of water welling up to eternal life."

How good that would be to my weary body and burning feet! I did not hesitate. "Sir, give me this water – so I won't get thirsty and have to keep coming here to draw water."

A strange hope began to stir within me.

"Go call your husband, and come back," He said.

Embarrassed and ashamed – I looked away. "I have no husband" I said.

"You are right when you say you have no husband", He said – and there was a kindness to His voice. He was not condemning me – or judging me. He was making me face myself and be honest – for the first time in a long time. "The fact is, you have had five husbands, and the man you now have is not your husband."

How could He know that? He was a stranger. But somehow, I did not feel exposed or humiliated – I felt relieved!

He must be a prophet I thought. So, I asked Him where and how we should worship. He told me that where we worship is not the important thing.

"God is spirit," He said, "and his worshipers must worship in the Spirit and in truth."

"I know that Messiah (called Christ) is coming," I said, "When he comes, he will explain everything to us."

"I, the one speaking to you – I am he," He said simply.

I was astonished! The Messiah – here? At my well? Talking so freely with me – such a sinful woman of Samaria? But it must be true – why else would my heart feel so clean, and my feet feel so light? I felt joy and hope bubbling up inside of me – just as he had said!

I forgot my purpose for coming to that well – left my still empty water pot there – and ran into town! I actually wanted to see all those people I had tried so hard to avoid!

"Come with me, everybody!" I shouted, tapping people on the shoulders as I skipped through the streets! "Come; see a man who told me everything I ever did. Could this be the Messiah?"

And follow me they did! They knew I was changed – completely!

Many believed because of my testimony – but many more believed because they came and saw and heard Him themselves!

Oh, I can never thank and praise Him enough for coming out of His way to me! His love and forgiveness brought the "living water" to my parched and empty soul. What a wonderful Savior!

He can do the same for you, my modern sister – He can do the same for you! You are precious to Him!

Chapter 24A:

Modern Woman – The Worldly Woman

*A*ctually, I'm comfortable and content with my life. We have a fine house in suburbia – close enough to the lights and lure of the big city. We've worked hard – and we're respected by our neighbors and others in the community. We have come into the soft lap of luxury – and I love it! Oh, it's not exactly something out of "Lifestyles of the Rich and Famous" – but it is cozy and warm – comforting, and comfortable! I want my children to grow up with all of these advantages – the good things in life that money can buy. Why shouldn't they have the best – they deserve it – we all do!

Oh, sure, once in a while I hear a different sound – a "still small voice" I think they say – calling me – tenderly – gently – "Follow me." And for a moment, I remember days gone by when my priorities in life were different. There was a certain peace I had in those days.

Oh – but who knows what that "follow me" may mean for me now – what changes I would have to make – what things I would have to give up – how my children might be deprived?

No – no! I know what I have now – I'm staying with the familiar, the snug and easy life I'm enjoying. Why should I have to sacrifice any of this to follow a way that might be hard and demanding?

Chapter 24B:

Response –
Remember Lot's Wife

Text: Genesis 19: 1-26

*O*h, sister – do not close your mind so quickly to His leading. This gentle voice you hear is yet another way He seeks to prove you are precious in His sight.

Believe me; I know how hard it is to leave a place – a lifestyle you love!

I remember when Lot first came to Sodom. He was different – an honest, upright man – God-fearing and strong. He really believed he could make a difference. But instead of Lot changing Sodom – Sodom changed Lot! The wickedness engulfed him, and while he was somewhat troubled by all the evil around him, he became numb to the things of God.

I occasionally remembered the times when we had worshiped and believed – Oh! But Sodom - with all of its shamefulness had a certain mystique and sensuousness that riveted me to it – its luxury and lure mesmerized me – I could never leave it!

And so, when the call came – when God sent two angels to lead us by the hand out of that city – away from impending death and destruction – they took me out of Sodom – but they could not take Sodom out of me! My heart was divided – my desire was different from the direction of my reluctant steps. Why should I leave? How could I give up that pleasure and prosperity – just one backward glance over my shoulder – even though the angel had warned against it......?

In that instant, the Sulphur and ash raining down from heaven entombed me – forever memorializing my forward feet and my reluctant glance.

Across the pages of time, I have become a monument to indecision.

How faithful God was to me! He gave me a chance to start anew – in the fresh, clean atmosphere of the mountains.

I could have been a monument to mercy because of God's opportunity for deliverance – but I chose to disobey! In trying to make the best of both worlds – I lost both. I died neither in Sodom nor on the mountain – but somewhere on the plain in between.

One wonders how the course of history might have been changed had I fully realized how precious I was to God – and how His grace had abounded toward me!

Oh my sister – do not ever be afraid to follow that "still small voice" – for therein is life – true life – abundant, full and eternal LIFE!

You are precious to Him – do not turn back from His calling to you!

SECTION VII- SPECIAL TOPICS

Chapter 25:

Heaven's Bread

(The Role of Bread in the Bible)

Texts: Exodus 16:4-5, 21-35; Exodus 39: 36;
Exodus 40:22,23; I Kings 17:7-16;
Judges 7: 8-15; Matthew 4: 1-4;
John 6: 1-13,25-59; Matthew 26: 17-30;
John 21: 1-14; Luke 24: 13-35;
I Corinthians 10: 14-17; Isaiah 55:2;
Psalm 34:8

Oh! You caught me making my morning bread – it's a daily thing you know! I suppose I could make it in my sleep! The recipe is as old as time – passed on from generation to generation. I remember my grandmother teaching me the fine art of mixing, kneading and shaping. Oh, the patience I learned in waiting for it to rise before baking it! And now, I try to teach my granddaughters – so they can teach their daughters and granddaughters.

Growing up, I often heard stories, told around the fire at night, about how God sent special bread down from Heaven. It was like dew every morning, and my ancestors would gather the day's supply as God directed – and the next day, there would be more! It was amazing! The people had never seen anything like it – and it sustained them for all those 40 years in the wilderness. Manna, they called it – meaning "What is it?" Oh, they complained because it wasn't onions, leeks and garlic like they had as slaves in Egypt – but God just kept supplying their "daily bread"!

And then there was the showbread – "The bread of the presence" – in the Tabernacle. It consisted of 12 loaves of unleavened bread, prepared and presented hot on the golden table every Sabbath. The loaves were square or oblong, and represented the twelve tribes of Israel. The old loaves were removed every Sabbath, and were to be eaten only by the priests in the court of the sanctuary. Once, David and his men ate it unlawfully, out of sheer hunger, when Saul was in pursuit of them.

Miracles have been associated with bread, too – like the time the prophet Elijah was sent to the widow at Zarephath. She was making a little fire, intending to prepare one last meal for herself and her son. After that, there would be no more food or supplies in the house – no more bread! Elijah told her to take the handful of flour she had left, and make HIM a small loaf of bread first – then to feed herself and her son. The widow did as the prophet asked, and the jar of flour and the cruse of oil lasted for many, many days – until the rains came again, and the crops were growing once more! Quite a faith that woman had to trust God to provide for her!

Oh and then there was the dream that Gideon overheard being described in the Midianite camp – a dream that a round loaf of barley bread came rolling down the hill and knocked over one of the Midianite tents! The man who was listening to the tale, said that it could mean only ONE thing – barley bread was the bread of poor people, and Gideon's army seemed poor and puny compared to the Midianites. So the barley bread represented the Israelites, and it meant they were going to roll right over those Midianites – even though there were hundreds MORE of them! It was a wonderful, comforting sign for Gideon that God would give his little army of 300 the victory over their enemy! Gideon went back to his camp, worshiped God, and then got everybody up with a shout – "Get up, the Lord has given the Midianite camp into your hands!"

What an exciting story – and BREAD was right there in the middle of if!

And then, came the man named Jesus. How He blessed and sanctified bread!

First, shortly after His baptism by John the Baptizer, Jesus was led away by the Spirit into the wilderness, where He fasted for 40 days and nights. During that time, the Devil came to Him – and tempted Him in three ways. One of those ways was the temptation to turn stones into bread! No doubt Jesus was very hungry at that point – and no doubt He could have done that quite easily – but instead, Jesus quoted the Word of God. "Man does not live on bread alone, but on every word that comes from the mouth of God."

My mother was in the crowd the day Jesus performed the greatest miracle with bread. She loved to tell me again and again how it all happened. A great crowd had been following Jesus wherever He went. They were so eager to hear His words that they would give Him no rest! On that day, they had stood for many hours in the heat of the day, with no food to eat. When Jesus presented the dilemma to His disciples, some wanted to just send the people away! Philip counted the cost, and determined that it would cost 200 days wages to feed everyone – and even then, they would not be filled! It was Andrew who went to work searching the crowd, and found a young lad with a little lunch, lovingly packed by his mother for the day's outing on the hillside. Andrew brought the lad to Jesus – then seemed to doubt that it would do much good after all! But the lad generously gave up his little lunch of five small barley loaves, and two tiny fish – and Jesus graciously received it! He lovingly blessed it, and then began to break it, and told his disciples to begin passing it out to the hungry crowd. The supply never ran out – until everyone had eaten until they were full – some 15 or 20 thousand people! And even then, it did not run out! Jesus told His followers to gather up the fragments that remained – and it filled twelve baskets! Each disciple had his own basket of leftovers for the next week – as a reminder of the Master's astounding miracle!

Many people followed Jesus after that in the hopes of seeing more signs and miracles. He finally told them plainly one day, "I am the Bread of Life – come down from Heaven. He who comes to me will never go hungry, and he who believes in me will never be thirsty." He also added, "This bread is my flesh, which I will give for the life of the world."

These were hard sayings for the people. They knew Jesus was the son of Joseph – how could He say He had come down from Heaven? And what was all this talk about eating His flesh?

Jesus was trying to prepare people for the real reason He had come – to be the Savior of the world, and to give His life as a ransom for many. There was something about Jesus "breaking the bread" that revealed His power and glory. Something in that simple act that opened people's eyes and helped them see who Jesus really was.

So many times in His short years of ministry, Jesus would go into the homes of the common people – Simon the Leper, Zacchaeus, Mary, Martha and Lazarus – and share a meal with them – and as they "broke the bread together" people's lives were changed and the glory of Jesus was revealed!

Finally, at the "last supper" – Jesus' final meal with his followers before His crucifixion – Jesus again took the bread, blessed and broke it, and told the twelve that it represented HIS BODY, which would be broken for them – soon! Just a few hours later, the disciples began to understand what He meant as their Master's broken body lay sealed in a borrowed tomb.

And then came that glorious Easter dawn, when the risen Jesus encountered women who had come to properly anoint His body – "Do not be afraid" He said, "It is I! Go tell my disciples that I have risen, and I go before them into Galilee."

There on that familiar shoreline as the grief-stricken followers floundered for fish – Jesus tenderly prepared breakfast for them – fish, and of course, BREAD! In the breaking of that bread, they beheld Him – recognized Him, and celebrated with Him the most glorious dawn of all time!

And who could forget those heavy-hearted travelers on the road to Emmaus? Confused and disillusioned by the events surrounding the cross, they numbly walked the familiar road toward home. A stranger joined them and listened to their sad recounting of the past few days' events. "We had hoped that He was the one who was going to redeem Israel", they said – about the VERY ONE who walked with them! It was not until they invited Him into their home, and He "broke the bread", that they recognized – JESUS! "Were not our hearts burning within us," they said, "while he talked with us on the road and opened the Scriptures to us?"

Jesus Christ – the Bread of Heaven – sent down not to SUSTAIN life – but to GIVE life. Someone has said that the unleavened bread is a picture of Jesus – it is round, symbolizing His eternity – no beginning and no ending. It is flat, signifying His humility in leaving Heaven to come to earth – and it is broken and shared around the table – just as His body was broken in death to give eternal life to all those who sit at His table!

And now, our brother Paul is telling us that WE are the body of Christ. We, His followers are to become the "living bread" to those without Christ. That means we must be willing to be broken and used for His sake. Sometimes, that brokenness comes in the form of a failure, a loss – a sorrow – a sickness. Whatever it takes, dear friends, we must be willing to BE Christ's broken bread – to yield our little all to the Master's hands, for Him to bless AND break – in order that His power and glory may be revealed through us! Nothing we give to Jesus is ever wasted!

"Why spend money on what it not bread, and your labor on what does not satisfy?" "Taste and see that the Lord is good!"

Chapter 26:

The Wedding Garment

(Being Properly Dressed for the Banquet)

**Text: Isaiah 61:10* (NKJV); Genesis 3: 21;
Deuteronomy 8: 2 – 4, 29:5;**

**I Samuel 17: 12 -51; Matthew 22: 1-14;
John 19: 23-24; Isaiah 64:6;
Revelation 7: 9-10* (NKJV)**

I am going to a wedding banquet – and I am ready! My lamp is trimmed – there is extra oil on hand – I am watching and waiting for the bridegroom! The preparations have been made – all things are now ready!

Most importantly, I am dressed in the wedding garment! I know it is the right one, because God Himself dressed me! Yes – it is true!

*"I will greatly rejoice in the Lord, My soul shall be joyful in my God; for He has clothed me with the garments of salvation- He has covered me with the robe of righteousness. As a bridegroom decks himself with ornaments and as a bride adorns herself with her jewels"...so the Lord Himself has dressed me up!

God has been dressing His forgiven people since the beginning of time, you know, going back to our first parents – Adam and Eve in the Garden of Eden. When they disobeyed God, they were suddenly aware of their nakedness, and tried to cover their shame with puny aprons of fig leaves sewn together! That must have been quite a sight! But even though God had to punish them for their disobedience – still He loved them – and just before He sent them out of the garden for good – He lovingly fashioned garments for them – and clothed them with animal skins.

The Word of God does not tell us what kind of animal it was – but some animal was sacrificed so that Adam and Eve could be covered with God's forgiveness and redemption! It was a sign of a far greater sacrifice that would happen hundreds of years later!

God dressed the children of Israel, too – with clothes and shoes that did not wear out for 40 years – as they wandered in the desert and the wilderness. Imagine! No wardrobe malfunction for 40 years – but then, no shopping either!

And then there was King David. Long before he was King – he was a simple shepherd boy taking morsels of food to his older brothers on the front line of battle – the Israelites against the Philistines. When David heard the giant Goliath roar across the valley, challenging anyone to come out and fight him, David volunteered to face the evil foe. King Saul hesitated – after all, David was just a lad up against a 9 foot giant! Then he had an idea. Saul decided to "dress up" David in his own suit of armor. Can you picture that? King Saul, who stood head and shoulders above any man in the kingdom – putting HIS armor on little David! Poor David said he could not even WALK in Saul's armor, let alone fight the giant!

David left the armor behind and stepped out to meet the giant dressed in the splendor of God's righteousness! "You come against me with a sword, a spear, and javelin," he said to Goliath, "but I come against you in the name of the Lord Almighty – the God of the armies of Israel whom you have defied….the battle is the Lord's" said David, "and He will give all of you into our hands!"

And with a simple stone and slingshot, David felled Goliath, and proved that God alone had dressed him for the battle!

Then came that glorious day when God pulled back the curtain of Heaven, said farewell to His only Son, and sent Jesus to earth clothed in humility and humanity and wrapped in swaddling cloths. He left behind His robes of glory and splendor – to walk earth's dusty roads, proclaiming God's eternal love for a fallen world.

Near the end of His life, as He gathered with His closet followers – He took off His outer garment and girded Himself with a towel and proceeded to wash everyone's feet! And the next day, that outer garment, now blood-stained and soiled with sweat and tears, lay in a heap at the foot of the cross upon which Jesus was crucified. Soldiers gambled for just a piece of that robe – a seamless robe – the only thing Jesus possessed in this world.

I have often thought of the soldiers who won that gamble – and took home that blood-stained cloth. How did they feel when they realized that Jesus had conquered death and was alive again? Did the souvenir haunt them? Did any of them seek Him out – desiring to exchange that tattered piece of robe for the robe of righteousness – the garment of salvation that Jesus had died to make possible for them? I wonder – oh, I wonder!

This was the sacrifice – once and for all – that had been foreshadowed in the Garden of Eden – when God so lovingly clothed Adam and Eve. Now, through Jesus' sacrifice on the cross, God has made it possible for every person to be dressed in His righteousness – His purity – His holiness!

While He was on earth, Jesus told many stories and parables, but I must tell you the one that changed my life forever!

Jesus said God's Kingdom is like a king who prepared a wedding banquet for His son. Not one of the invited guests came to the feast – in fact, they beat and killed the messengers who brought them the invitation.

The King immediately instructed his servants to go out to the busiest intersections of the city and invite anyone and everyone to the wedding banquet – for everything was ready!

And so, the rag-tag folks came in – and at the door, each surprised guest received a wedding garment for the rags they were wearing. The guests were not forced to wear the new robe, but NOT to wear it showed a lack of respect and appreciation to the King who had sacrificed to make the garment possible!

When the King arrived at the banquet, he saw there a man without the wedding garment, even though one had been provided for him.

"How did you get in here without wedding clothes, friend?" the King asked. The man could not say a word, for he knew the garment had been provided for him and he had deliberately chosen not to wear it!

The King ordered his servants to bind him, hand and foot – take him away and cast him into outer darkness, where there will be weeping and gnashing of teeth.

When I heard Jesus tell this story, I knew it was about me! I saw myself there at that wedding feast.

I was there, but without the wedding garment God had provided for me. I was a hypocrite, trying to hide in the crowd, and I knew my disguise would soon be stripped off. God knows who are right in their hearts and who are not. We may deceive one another, but we can never deceive Him!

I learned that when I "put on" Jesus – that is when I accepted His love and His sacrifice into my heart – when He became my all in all – I received my wedding garment!

My self-righteous acts were never anything more than a shabby garment. "Filthy rags" the prophet Isaiah said. How disgusting were my own filthy, rotten garments – barely covering my naked shame!

How I needed to be clothed with His grace! I could not buy this garment – for Jesus had already bought it for me! I could not clean it myself, for it had to be washed in the blood of the Lamb. There was nothing I could do to earn it – I don't deserve it – but I CAN wear it – Hallelujah! God dressed me in it – and I one day can join the countless millions who will come into God's presence dressed in His righteousness that Jesus purchased for me, on the cross of Calvary!

Oh my dear friends – we are all invited to the wedding banquet! Jesus is the bridegroom and we, His followers – His church – are the Bride! Make no mistake – your garments must be as white as snow! No other mode or code of dress will get you to the Wedding Feast in Heaven.

* "After these things I looked, and behold, a great multitude which no one could number, of all nations, tribes, peoples and tongues, standing before the throne and before the Lamb clothed with white robes with palm branches in their hands, and crying out with a loud voice saying – 'Salvation belongs to our God who sits on the throne, and to the Lamb!' "

Oh, they will come from the east – from the west – from the north – from the south – and sit down together in God's Kingdom! The rich – the poor – the hated – the troubled – will sit together at God's banquet table! No one will question their past – their sin – their robes will be spotless, white and clean! Yes, they'll come from every land – every nation – every tribe – and sit down together in the Kingdom of God!

Behold! The Bridegroom comes! Ah, sisters rise up – be watchful – be ready – and let God dress you up for the wedding!

Chapter 27:

Tracing His Steps

(Reflections of Mary the Mother of Jesus)

Texts: Luke 2:41-50(MSG); Matthew 3:17 (NKJV); John 1:34b(NKJV)

Matthew 4:1-22;John 2:1-11; Luke 7:36-50; Acts 1:9-12(NIV)

I remember the first time I saw His feet – pink, soft, tiny. I held them in my hand as He lay in the crook of my arm. Like every new mother before me, and after me, I counted the toes to be sure they were perfect. I had felt those feet many times kicking against the wall of my womb – but now to SEE them – it struck my heart – these are the feet of God – Immanuel's feet – "God with us!" This baby I had been carrying for nine months was God's Son—our Redeemer – Jesus! Suddenly, I was smitten again with awe and humility – to be part of such a miracle. As I caressed those tiny feet, I was also reminded of the responsibility that was mine to raise and nurture this child. This was no ordinary baby – still, I had been chosen to be His mother – to hold Him, rock Him, feed Him, and teach Him – to care for Him during His growing years. It would have been overwhelming except I knew I would not be doing it all alone. Not only would my dear Joseph be by my side, but God Himself! The power of the Highest would hover over me. That's what the angel Gabriel had said, and I believed it!

Those tiny feet grew quickly and like every little boy, Jesus loved to run and jump and play, to climb a tree – to skip through the fields. He followed me to the market, to the well, to Joseph's carpenter shop, and ah, yes! To the Synagogue! How He devoured the Rabbi's teaching. How He loved the Scriptures – and memorized them. "It is written" He would often say – as if He had written it Himself – or had some part in it!

When He was twelve, we made our annual pilgrimage to Jerusalem for the Feast of the Passover. It was always a joyous time for Jesus – running ahead on happy feet with His brothers, His cousins and friends. He loved being with people. When the feast was over and we were headed home to Nazareth, Jesus stayed behind, but we did not know it. We thought He was with friends or family as usual. But after an entire day's travel on foot,

He did not come to us that night. We began to search for Him – to ask everyone we met if they had seen Him. Feelings of fear and anger collided inside my heart and grew stronger with each step we took back toward Jerusalem. The next day, we found Him in the Temple, seated among the teachers, listening to them, and asking questions. The teachers were astonished at His questions and His answers. Relief and resentment consumed me – "Young man," I scolded, "Why have you done this to us? Your father and I have been half out of our minds looking for you."(MSG)

"Why were you looking for me?" He asked. "Did you not know that I had to be here dealing with the things of my Father?"(MSG)

Joseph and I looked at each other in bewilderment. What did this mean? I had that long, dusty walk home to consider it all – and with each step I took, it became clearer to me – those precious young feet were destined for greater things and would not be under my roof forever. This I held in my heart every day after that!

Jesus continued to grow up and the favor of God was upon Him. He learned the skill of His carpenter father, but He also loved to talk with the fishermen, the merchants, the farmers and the shepherds. Even as a young man, He seemed to have a heart for the poor. He would stop to talk with a beggar by the road – or run to help the widow carry her load. One day, with his young feet dragging, He tenderly, tearfully buried a dead sparrow in a shallow grave He dug behind our home.

And then one day, it happened. Jesus walked away from our Nazareth home with resoluteness on His face. He never looked back, and I knew in my heart that His real mission to earth had begun. He walked to the Jordan River that day, and insisted that His cousin, John the Baptizer should baptize Him. With great reluctance, John finally complied, and immediately, the heavens opened, and the Holy Spirit in a bodily form like a dove, descended and came to rest on His head. And then, a voice that shook the very foundation of the earth declared – "This is my beloved Son, in whom I am well pleased!" As many people stood there transfixed by what they had seen and heard, John's voice rang out with authority – "This is the Son of God!"

"Yes – Yes!" my heart cried! At last, the secret I had carried for thirty years was now declared for all to hear! My feet barely stayed on the ground as I watched my son – God's Son – receive the affirmation of His heavenly Father. Surely all of Israel would rejoice to know that Messiah had come! Surely there could be no doubt or questions now as to who this Nazarene truly was. Little did I know that some in that crowd were already angry and jealous – seething within themselves. They would never believe – they would never follow – they would never know.

Almost immediately, Jesus was led by the Holy Spirit into the wilderness, where He was tempted by Satan. Forty days He stayed there – fasting, praying – resisting the evil one. The angels took care of Him there in that desert, and when He returned, the glory of God was on His face, and in His feet! Jesus walked back into town and changed the world forever!

He walked along the shores of His beloved Galilee and spoke a simple calling to the fishermen there. "Follow Me," He said, and they did – leaving nets and boats and livelihoods behind to walk with Him. Tax collectors and carpenters, publicans and prostitutes, mothers, fathers and ah, yes – children! They were drawn to Him – to listen to Him talk – to walk the way He walked.

It was amazing to see crowds following Him – along dusty roads and the grassy hillsides. Ordinary, everyday people were standing for hours – walking for miles – just to hear His words. Oh, but I knew in my heart He was capable of so much more. The angel Gabriel had told me He would be great, and do mighty things. Surely there would be signs and wonders and MIRACLES! After all, He was the Son of GOD!

So, when we attended a family wedding in Cana – I suggested that he DO something to help the embarrassed host when the wine ran out at the wedding feast.

("Dear) woman," He said to me," why do you involve me? My hour has not yet come."

That is what he SAID, but I could read something different in His eyes. A readiness – a willingness – a twinkle! I slipped quietly toward the servants. "Do whatever He tells you," I encouraged them.

Soon I saw Jesus moving toward them, talking with them. They scurried to fill the six large stone water jars nearby. I watched with excitement as they filled each one to the brim. Then they began dipping it out, and serving it to the guests, beginning with the host. He received it reluctantly – then took a sip. A smile of delight lit up his face as he licked his lips and called to the bridegroom. "Everyone brings out the choice wine first and then the cheaper wine after the guests have had too much to drink; but you have saved the best till now!"

It was amusing to see the bewildered look on the bridegroom's face! Then, he just nodded and smiled as if he had planned the whole thing! Soon every table was buzzing with laughter and conversation about this "water turned to wine." Oh, how I was enjoying that moment! When suddenly, Jesus came from behind me, picked me up off my feet and twirled me around and around! Then we danced and danced and celebrated together His first MIRACLE!

From that time on, there were many miracles! People fell at His feet, begging Him for healing or help of some sort – and help He did! He healed lepers, blind men, bent over women, demon possessed men, women and children. The lame walked again – the deaf heard and yes, in some cases, the dead were raised to life again! He multiplied a small boy's lunch to feed thousands, calmed a storm at sea, and with those precious feet, walked on the waters of Galilee to comfort His terrified followers. He wasn't afraid to dirty His feet on the dusty roads of Samaria, Capernaum, Jerusalem, and countless tiny villages in between. Everywhere He went, He condemned the injustices of the powerful and haughty, and rewarded the simple, true faith of the poor.

One evening, as He dined with friends and followers at the home of one Simon, a Pharisee, a sinful woman boldly broke into the party and began weeping at Jesus' feet, as He reclined at the table. She washed His feet with her tears, wiped them with her hair, kissed them, and anointed them with perfume. This caused quite a stir and Jesus was promptly criticized for letting this sinful woman even touch Him!

He saw her humble act as one of faith and supreme love. He scolded the host for failing to wash His feet or anoint them. He had even failed to greet Jesus with the customary welcome kiss. Yet, this broken woman had done it all. Jesus saw her heart, forgave her sins, and sent her away filled with the peace she had been longing for!

Anger and opposition mounted against Jesus, and He began to speak often about His coming suffering and death. Surely I did not want to hear those words. He was still so young – so much life ahead of Him. Still, those words spoken by Simeon haunted me – "A sword will pierce your own soul too..." Was this what he meant?

At the Passover feast that year, Jesus shared a meal in a private upper room with His closest followers. John told me later that Jesus had said one of them would betray Him into the hands of sinners. But before He said that, He had done a beautiful thing – He laid aside the seamless robe I had made for Him – girded Himself with a towel, and washed the feet of each of His disciples. He said that no servant is greater than His master and that WE should wash one another's feet – that is, humbly serve one another!

That night, He WAS betrayed, arrested, tried, beaten and convicted, all within a few short hours. By early the next morning, His bruised and bleeding feet were stumbling along the Via Dolorosa – the way of the cross. That sword spoken of by Simeon truly did pierce through my heart as I watched them nail those precious feet and hands to a rough cross of execution! Flashbacks filled my mind of all the places those sacred feet had traveled – all the times those feet had carried Him to teach, to preach, to heal, to forgive, cleanse and save the people He loved enough to stay nailed and impaled on that cross for!

Surely this could not be the end. His kingdom was to last forever! That's what Gabriel had told me.

The first day of the week, some of the women went back to the tomb were Jesus had been buried. They had gone to anoint His body. But when they arrived, the stone sealing the tomb had been rolled back and the tomb was empty! Mary of Magdala wept in despair as she supposed someone had stolen His body. Suddenly, someone spoke her name with such tender love! "Rabboni!" she said, as she ran to Him and fell at His feet! He had risen – just as He said! Hallelujah!

I saw Him many times during the next forty days. His body was glorified – Oh, but I KNEW it was Him!

Then one day He led us out to the vicinity of Bethany. He lifted up His hands and blessed us – and while He was blessing us, He left us, and was taken up into Heaven. Oh, if ever I wanted to hold on to His feet – to keep Him with me – it was then! But I knew His earthly ministry was done – He had accomplished the work His Heavenly Father had sent Him to do. Two angels appeared to us – "Why do you stand here looking into the sky?" they asked us – "This same Jesus, who has been taken from you into Heaven, will COME BACK in the same way you have seen Him go into Heaven!"

And so, He is coming back – my Son – God's Son – my Savior! And until then.....we MUST follow – keep following in His steps!

Chapter 28:

What is that in Your Hand?

(A Challenge to use what God gives you)

**Texts: Joshua 6:17-25; II Kings 4:1-7;
Matthew 26:7-13; Acts 9: 36-42**

**(A dialogue between God
and some women of the Bible)**

GOD: Rahab, what is that in your hand? (A voice off stage)

RAHAB: - O, this, Lord? It's just a piece of string – a cord – a scarlet cord!

GOD: - Will you give it to me, Rahab?

RAHAB: - Give it to YOU? Well – uh – yes, of course, Lord, I'll give it to You!

NARRATOR: And Rahab took that scarlet cord, and bound it to her window, as the spies sent from Joshua told her to do. And because of her faith and obedience, she and all of her family were spared when the city of Jericho was destroyed.

When she gave that cord to God – a wonderful thing happened.....it became the cord of SALVATION, and Rahab was part of a miracle!!

(PAUSE)

GOD: - Widow, what is that in your hand?

WIDOW: - Oh, this, Lord? It's just a little cruse of oil – it's all I've got left in my house – not much, really!

GOD: - Will you give it to me, widow?

WIDOW: - Give it to YOU? Well – uh – yes, of course, Lord, I'll give it to You!

NARRATOR: - And the widow obeyed God, and gathered all sorts of empty vessels from her friends and neighbors – every kind and size of container she could possibly find. Then when she had gathered them all, she shut the door, and took that little curse of oil, and filled every container she had! The oil was sold, her debts were paid, and her sons were spared from being sold as slaves!

When she gave the oil to God – a wonderful thing happened.....it became the oil of SUBMISSION..... and that widow was part of a miracle!

(PAUSE)

GOD: - Mary, what is that in your hand?

MARY: - Oh, this, Lord? It's just a little bottle of perfume – it WAS expensive, but it's still not very much!

GOD: - Will you give it to me, Mary?

MARY: - Give it to YOU, Lord? Well, - uh – yes, of course, Lord, I'll give it to You!

NARRATOR: - And Mary broke that precious alabaster jar of perfume and anointed the head and feet of Jesus, to the dismay and disgust of those others present. They spoke about such waste, and how the perfume could be sold, and the money given to the poor. But Jesus accepted it as a beautiful outpouring of love and devotion to Him, said she had done a beautiful thing, and had really anointed Him for His burial!

When she gave the perfume to God, a wonderful thing happened! It became the perfume of SINCEREITY – and Mary was part of a miracle!

(PAUSE)

GOD: - Dorcas, what is that in your hand?

DORCAS: - O, this, Lord? It's just a needle and thread, that's all, nothing special!

GOD: - Will you give it to me, Dorcas?

DORCAS: - Give it to YOU? Well, uh – yes, Lord, of course, I'll give it to You!

NARRATOR: - And with that needle and thread, Dorcas made garments and tunics for the followers of Christ, and their families. Made them with love – so many of them! Suddenly, she died, and the women came to Peter, bearing the robes and garments she had made, weeping and mourning her death. Peter went to where her body was, took her by the hand, and restored her to life and health!

When Dorcas gave her needle and thread to God, a wonderful thing happened. It became the needle of SERVICE, and Dorcas was part of a miracle!

(PAUSE)

GOD: - And what about YOU,_____, and YOU_____

NARRATOR: and you, and you, and YOU!

GOD: - What is in YOUR hand?

NARRATOR: - Yes, what is it? Does it seem small –
insignificant – unimportant??

GOD: - Will you give it to me?

NARRATOR: - When you give it to God – a wonderful thing will happen – and YOU can be part of
a MIRACLE!

> A miracle for You and Me?
> It surely can be true –
> For the miracle's not in what we have,
> But in WHO we give it to!
> What is it, right there in YOUR hand –?
> Hidden deep within?
> Just give it to the Master,
> And the miracle will begin!

Study Guide

The following study guide for each chapter is meant to simply be a guide toward discussion and further thought about each character and story.

It can be used for individual study, or in a group setting such as a Bible study. The questions included are suggested to stimulate conversation and dialogue, and help readers to dig a little deeper into God's Word!

Chapter 1: - The Baby in a Basket

TEXTS: Exodus 1: 1-2:10; 15: 1-2

1. What touched you the most from this chapter?
2. Did the midwives lie to Pharaoh? How is that justified?
3. What was the most outstanding thing about Jochebed's faith?

4. *Why do you think Pharaoh's daughter did not carry out her father's orders and kill Moses?*
5. *What were some of the unexpected outcomes when Pharaoh's daughter found the baby?*
6. *Compare Exodus 1:15-22 with Matthew 2: 1-18. Discuss.*
7. *How do these massacres compare to the "baby killings" in our country today?*
8. *How was Moses a picture of the Deliverer to come – Jesus, our Savior?*
9. *What are the similarities between Moses and Jesus?*
10. *What are the differences?*
11. *How did God raise up a friend for His people even among their enemies?*
12. *Tell of a time you or someone you know had to give a child back to God.*
13. *Why do you think 3 great leaders came from Jochebed's family?*

PRAYER TOPIC:

Pray about the practice of abortion that goes on in our country – praying especially for those who perform the abortions – (that God would bring conviction to their hearts). Pray for the women who have had abortions. Pray for our government leaders and frontline organizations that are taking a strong stand against abortion, that God will keep them strong and courageous. Pray for any girls/ women who may even now be considering abortion.

Chapter 2 – Mary's Joy

TEXT: Luke 1: 1-38

1. How did Mary receive the news that she was to bear God's Son?
2. Have you ever had an encounter with an angel? Share your story!
3. Did Mary hesitate or ask for a few days to think it over? Why or why not?
4. God delights in doing impossible things! Read Joshua 3:5;

Psalm 77:14 Discuss.

5. What impossible situations are you facing?
6. Why is doing God's will always best for us?

PRAYER TOPIC:

Pray for those who right now are facing some decision regarding their future – or some seemingly impossible situation. Ask God to give them His peace and divine direction as they seek to align their lives with His will.

Chapter 3:- Mary's Journey

TEXTS: Luke 1: 39-56

1. How did Elizabeth know Mary was with child?
2. How did she know this baby was the Messiah?
3. Why was Mary's visit to Elizabeth so important to Mary?
4. What was the beautiful gift Elizabeth gave to her?
5. Encouragement is something we all need. Read and discuss the following Scripture portions: Proverbs 10:21, 12:25, 15:23, 16:24 and Isaiah 50:4
6. How do you think Elizabeth's encouragement helped Mary?

PRAYER TOPIC:

Pray for those around you right now who need encouragement or affirmation in their lives. Put legs on your prayers and go encourage them yourself – give hugs – write a note – call them on the phone – take them to lunch! Ask God to lead you to someone who needs your encouragement today!

Chapter 4: - Mary's Judgment
TEXT: Matthew 1: 18-25

The Bible doesn't tell us much about the ridicule and judgment awaiting Mary when she returned to Nazareth after visiting Elizabeth for three months – but we can be sure it was very real and frightening for this young girl, Mary.

1. How does our Scripture give us a clue about the judgment Mary was facing when she returned home?
2. How did this chapter help you to appreciate Joseph?
3. Read and discuss Romans 8: 31-39
4. How does it help us to know that God is FOR us?
5. How did Joseph's dream assure Mary that God was for her?
6. Tell of a time when you were misjudged or wrongfully accused. How did this make you feel? Share your story!
7. How can we stand against the tide that is rising against Christians in our world today?

PRAYER TOPIC:

Pray for those who are being judged unfairly, ridiculed and belittled. Many around the world and even in our own country are being arrested, imprisoned and fined for taking a stand for Christ. Pray that God will keep them strong and that others will come alongside to stand with them.

Chapter 5:- Mary's Jesus

TEXT: Luke 2: 1 -35

1. How must the journey to Bethlehem been for Mary?
2. Why were so many people in Bethlehem at this time?
3. Have you ever been traveling and could not find a place to sleep overnight? Share your story!
4. How did you feel during that experience?
5. Was the fact that Jesus was born in a stable or cave the fault of the Innkeeper? Why or why not?
6. Why do you think God chose such a lowly surrounding for His Son's birthplace?
7. Where is the BEST place to give Jesus room?
8. Read the following Scripture portions and discuss – Proverbs 4:23; Matthew 15: 18-20; Psalm 51:10; Romans 10: 9-10; I John 4:15
9. What does the name Jesus mean? Why do you think God chose that name?
10. Why was it hard for Mary to "let go" of Jesus?

PRAYER TOPIC:

Pray for those who have not made room in their hearts for the Lord Jesus, but instead crowd Him out with their own plans, activities, relationships and agendas.

Chapter 6: - The Innkeeper's Wife

TEXTS: Luke 2: 1-40; Matthew 2: 1-23; Luke 23: 26-43

Much of chapter 6 is fiction – the character herself is not mentioned in the Bible – but on the other hand, we cannot rule out the possibility that someone like her really did exist!

1. *What did you like about this story? How did it touch/impact you?*
2. *Why do you think God chose the shepherds to receive the "good news" that night?*
3. *How does their reaction speak to us?*
4. *What was the significance of the Magi gifts of gold, frankincense, and myrrh?*
5. *In this story, why was Leah relieved to hear what her son said from the cross?*
6. *And why was she even MORE relieved when she heard what Jesus said to her son?*
7. *How can we comfort people whose children are not serving the Lord?*

PRAYER TOPIC:

Pray for those who have wayward children who are not serving the Lord. Pray for those who are incarcerated for crimes they have committed. Pray for those who have come to know Christ while in prison, that their faith may remain bold and strong.

Chapter 7: - Don't Miss the Party

TEXT: Luke 15: 11-32

1. Describe how those parents must have felt, watching their son walk away from home and all that represented for him.
2. Why is it important to pray for our children even long after they have left home?
3. How does praying for our children help us?
4. Who did the son say he had sinned against? Why is this important to note?
5. What was he willing to do in order to come home?
6. This is a story Jesus told – what do you think are the lessons He is teaching here?
7. Read the following Scripture portions and discuss: Psalm 78:38, 84:11; John 1:16; Romans 1:5, 5:17; Ephesians 1: 7-8. How do these verses relate to the story?
8. Why is forgiveness such a part of this story?

PRAYER TOPIC:

Pray for parents with broken hearts because of prodigal children. Pray for parents who cannot seem to forgive their children when they come "home." Pray for all families that are fractured because of sin and/or unforgiveness.

Chapter 8: - Room at the Table

TEXTS: Luke 14: 15-24; Isaiah 55:1

1. What grabbed your attention, your heart in this story?
2. What is the "banquet" the Lord has invited us to attend?
3. Have you ever given the Lord excuses for not answering His invitation? How did that go for you?
4. Why is it important to note the Master's anger in this story?
5. Is it always convenient to answer the Lord's call? Why or why not?
6. What could happen if we wait for it to be convenient for us?
7. This is a story Jesus told – what is the lesson in it for us today?

PRAYER TOPIC:

Pray for the outcasts and misfits of our day – the broken, the hurting, and the lonely. Let us ask God to help us to reach out to them with God's gracious invitation for them!

Chapter 9: - Mary of Bethany

**TEXTS: Luke 10: 38-42; John 11: 1, 5;
Matthew 26: 7-13; Mark 14: 3-9:
John 11: 2, 12:3**

1. What particularly touched or blessed you from this story?
2. Do you think it was easy for Mary to publically display her special love for Jesus by the anointing? Why or why not?
3. How was she criticized?
4. Have you ever been criticized for some act of love you thought you were giving to the Lord? Share your story!
5. Why did Jesus say to "leave her alone"?
6. Her anointing was symbolic of what coming event?
7. What are some ways we could "pour out" our love for Jesus?

PRAYER TOPIC:

Pray for those who are shy about serving Jesus. Some may feel that because they don't have the gift of preaching or teaching or singing, that they are not useful in His service. Ask God to help you appreciate those "alabaster boxes" that people have – like those who visit or send cards or always work in the church kitchen, or offer to take their turn in the nursery. Remember those "behind the scenes" gifts are just as important to Jesus as the more public ones!

Chapter 10: - Mary of Magdala

TEXTS: Matthew 15:39; Mark 16:9; Luke 8: 2-3; Matthew 27:56; Mark 15:40; John 19:25; Matthew 27:61, 28:8-10; John 20: 14-18

1. Were you surprised to learn that Mary of Magdala was not a prostitute or a woman of "ill repute"? She has been much misunderstood!
2. How did her condition affect her daily life?
3. Do you think demon possession is still a problem in our world today?
4. Have you ever encountered a demon possessed person? Share your story!
5. Why do you think Mary stayed all the while with Jesus at the cross?
6. What was the message Jesus entrusted Mary to give to others?
7. What are some of the ways we can resist the devil?
8. Read the following Scripture portions and discuss: Ephesians 4:27; Hebrews 2: 10-15; Ephesians 6: 10-17; James 4:7
9. Do we have access to the same power Mary Magdalene experienced from Jesus?

PRAYER TOPIC:

Pray for all those who are being held captive by Satan in spiritual bondage. Pray that they may see the power of Jesus revealed and claim the freedom *they can have through Him. Pray for the sex-traders and the drug dealers that the power of Satan will be broken in their lives. Pray for all those who minister to people who are bound by those sins.*

Chapter 11: - Jared's Lunch

TEXTS: Matthew 14: 15-21; Mark 6: 35-44; Like 9: 12-17; John 6: 1-66; Psalm 34:8

1. What was the mother's attitude in the beginning?
2. How did that change when Jared returned home and recounted the story of the miracle involving his lunch?
3. Jesus had a great crowd of followers after this, but what were they interested in?
4. What is the food which lasts on into eternal life?
5. What do you think Jesus meant when He said, "I am the bread of life"?
6. What angered the Jews when Jesus said He was the true bread that came down from Heaven?
7. Compare John 6: 51, 53-58 with Luke 22: 14-20. Discuss
8. Why did people turn away from following Jesus after His discussion with them as recorded in John 6?

PRAYER TOPIC:

Pray for people who have turned aside from Jesus – for those who find His sayings too hard for them to accept. Pray for those who are spiritually hungering, but are making the wrong choices in an effort to satisfy their hunger.

Chapter 12: - Claudia Procula

TEXT: Matthew 27: 11-31

1. Why was Claudia Procula troubled and sleepless?
2. What do you think her dream might have been?
3. Why didn't Pilate listen to her advice in the note she sent?
4. What things keep people from following Jesus?
5. What keeps you from standing up for Jesus?
6. How might the story have been different if Pilate and Claudia had gone to Calvary?
7. What should Pilate have done instead of washing his hands?

PRAYER TOPIC:

Pray for those who "put off" following Jesus. Pray for those who fear the crowd and are afraid to stand up against the tide of popular opinion in order to follow Jesus.

Chapter 13: - I've Just Seen Jesus

TEXTS: John 1:29; Matthew 5: 1-12; Matthew Chapters 5-7; Matthew 20: 20-28; Mark 15:40, 16:1, 2; Matthew 20: 18, 19, 28: 1-10

1. What did James and John do for a living before Jesus called them to follow Him?
2. Did they hesitate when the call came? Why or why not?
3. Why do you think they were called the "Sons of Thunder"? See Mark 3:17; Luke 9:51-56 – Discuss.
4. What was Salome's request for her sons?
5. What do you think prompted that request?
6. What did Jesus say we should do if we want to be great in His Kingdom?
7. In what ways did Jesus show He was a servant?
8. Share about someone you know who is a true servant of Jesus.

PRAYER TOPIC:

Pray for ourselves, that we may be willing to be servants of Christ – serving others humbly in His name. Pray for those who are humbly serving Christ in lonely, forgotten places around the world.

Chapter 14: - Dinner Guest in Emmaus

TEXTS: John 8: 2-59, 9:1-41; Luke 24: 13-35

1. What do you think the atmosphere of Jerusalem was like between Palm Sunday and Good Friday?
2. Why were so many people angry with Jesus?
3. Describe the events on the "Emmaus Road" returning from Jerusalem
4. Why do you think Jesus was recognized when He broke the bread at dinner that night?
5. Have you ever had an "Emmaus Road" experience – when you were burdened and heavy-hearted, nearly hopeless – and Jesus showed up? Share your story!
6. How do we keep a "burning heart" toward Jesus?
7. Read Psalm 34: 17-18. Discuss

PRAYER TOPIC:

Pray for those you know who are traveling along the road of life discouraged, despondent and seemingly without hope. Pray that someone (perhaps even YOU) will come alongside them and point them to Jesus!

Chapter 15: - Elisha and the Widow's Oil

TEXT: II Kings 4: 1-7

1. How was the creditor impacted by the miracle in this story?
2. How did God provide for the widow beyond her immediate need?
3. How did the widow show her faith?
4. Is God concerned about our financial and material needs?
5. Has God ever supplied a financial/material need for you in a miraculous way? Share your story!
6. Read Matthew 6:25-34. Discuss

PRAYER TOPIC:

Pray for those who are struggling financially, and for those in other parts of the world who have little of this world's goods. Pray for the homeless and disadvantaged in your own community. Pray for the widows you know, and ask God to show you ways to help and encourage them.

Chapter 16: - The Healing of Naaman

TEXT: II Kings 5:1-14

1. How were people with leprosy treated in Bible days?
2. In what ways was Naaman affected by this disease?
3. Who is the key person in the story that led Naaman to his eventual healing?
4. Why do you think Elisha didn't just come out and heal Naaman on the spot?
5. What else did Naaman have to be healed of besides leprosy?
6. How do you think the servant girl knew Elisha could heal Naaman when he had never healed anyone of leprosy before?
7. God used the little servant girl to be the messenger that led to a miracle. Can God us you, too? Discuss the possibilities!
8. Not everyone is literally healed from a disease they have – but what is more important than physical healing?
9. How do we cope with the fact that not everyone is healed?

PRAYER TOPIC:

Pray for those who are facing a long road of treatment and sickness because of cancer. Pray for all those who are caring for people with terminal illnesses or debilitating conditions. Pray for people who still struggle with the disease of leprosy.

Chapter 17: - The Raising of Lazarus

TEXT: John 11:1-44

1. Why were Mary and Martha disappointed with Jesus?
2. Why do you think Jesus delayed coming to them when He first got word that Lazarus was sick?
3. Why did Jesus weep at the tomb, when He knew He was going to raise Lazarus back to life?
4. Describe the emotions that would have been exhibited in the crowd that witnessed this resurrection.
5. Why did this miracle further anger the Jewish leaders against Jesus?
6. How can Jesus bring comfort and hope even if our loved one is not raised back to life? Share your story!

PRAYER TOPIC:

Pray for those who have recently lost loved ones – family members or friends. Pray that Jesus will draw near with His comfort and peace.

Chapter 18: - Midnight Praises

TEXT: Acts 16: 16-34

1. Who was troubling Paul and Silas in the streets?
2. Why were Paul and Silas arrested?
3. Why were Paul and Silas able to sing praises to God at midnight after being beaten and put into stocks in prison?
4. Have you ever been falsely accused? Describe how that felt.
5. Were you still able to praise God? Why or why not? Share your story!
6. Why was the jailer so frightened after the earthquake?
7. Why was he going to take his own life?
8. Why didn't Paul and Silas just walk out of the prison?
9. What was God's greater purpose in all this?
10. How did Paul and Silas answer the jailer when he asked, "What must I do to be saved?" Discuss the answer

PRAYER TOPIC:

Pray for those who are even now imprisoned wrongfully because of their faith in Jesus Christ. Pray for their spouses and family members at home. Pray for those individuals and organizations that are working for their release.

Chapter 19: - A Miracle in Cana

TEXT: John 2: 1-11

1. How was a wedding in the day of Christ different than one we would attend today?
2. Why do you think Mary approached Jesus about the wine shortage?
3. It seems on the surface that Jesus was somewhat abrupt with His mother. Discuss.
4. Do you think Jesus "changed His mind" or that He intended to do the miracle all along?
5. What showed that Mary believed Jesus would do the miracle?
6. Why do you think Jesus chose this miracle as His first?
7. Is it less dramatic or important than healing the blind or the lame?
8. Does it surprise you that Jesus would even go to this party? Why or why not?
9. Does Jesus want us to have good times – fun times in this life? How do we know that?

PRAYER TOPIC:

Pray for those who have recently been married. Pray for those in our nation who dare to take a stand for traditional marriage – between one man and one woman. Pray for those businesses and organizations that are being fined and maligned because they uphold the Biblical design for marriage. Pray for those who are struggling in their marriage and for those who have an unsaved spouse.

Chapter 20 A&B

Modern Woman: The Diagnosis – Response: Woman with the Issue of Blood

TEXTS: Matthew 9:18-22; Mark 5:21-34; Luke 8:40-48

1. How are these two women alike?
2. How are they different?
3. What were the social and religious restrictions imposed on the Biblical woman because of her illness?
4. How did she show her faith?
5. Why was this a huge risk for her?
6. How did Jesus know someone had touched Him?
7. Why did Jesus call her "daughter"?
8. How can we touch Him today since He is no longer here physically?

PRAYER TOPIC:

Pray for those who have been struggling with debilitating illnesses for a long time. Pray for those who are overlooked or cast aside be society because of some physical condition over which they have no control.

Chapter 21 A&B

Modern Woman: The New Widow – Response: The Widow and Her Cruse of Oil

TEXT: II Kings 4: 1-7

1. *How are these two women alike?*
2. *How are they different?*
3. *What did the widow in the Bible do to help herself?*
4. *What are some of the ways she showed her faith?*
5. *What hope can we offer to people who are facing financial crisis?*
6. *What can we do for those who have lost a spouse?*
7. *What advice could we give the modern woman?*

PRAYER TOPIC:

Pray for those in your church, neighborhood or workplace who have recently lost their spouse through death – or divorce. Pray that the Lord will show you ways you can help, encourage and minister to them.

Chapter 22 A&B

Modern Woman: The Lost Son – Response: The Shunemite Woman

TEXT: II Kings 4: 8-37

1. How are these two women alike?
2. How are they different?
3. What hope can we give the modern woman whose son has walked away from the life style and values of his parents?
4. What shows the faith and commitment of the Shunemite woman before her child was born? And after he died?
5. Name all of the brave attributes of this woman
6. How was she able to say "all is well" when it certainly was not?
7. What is the best thing we can do to help restore our children to a right relationship with God?
8. What can we take away from this story?

PRAYER TOPIC:

Pray for those parents who have children who have strayed far from the Christian principles and values they grew up with. Pray for the children – that God will bring to their minds what they were taught about God when they were growing up.

Chapter 23 A&B

Modern Woman: The Ashamed Woman – Response: The Samaritan Woman

TEXT: John 4: 1-42

1. *How are these two women alike?*
2. *How are they different?*
3. *How do we know the woman of Samaria had not found satisfaction in her life?*
4. *What was surprising to her about Jesus' approach to her? Name several things*
5. *Why did she go to the well in the heat of the day?*
6. *Why did this woman want the water Jesus was offering to her?*
7. *Why do you think Jesus chose to reveal His true identity and mission to this one lone woman? How does that encourage us?*
8. *Why did the woman go back into town and talk to the very people she was trying to avoid by coming to the well at midday?*
9. *What was the result of her doing that?*
10. *How should we treat a woman like that who may live in our neighborhood, worship at our church or work at our workplace?*

PRAYER TOPIC:

Pray for those who have suffered physical or sexual abuse as children. Pray for those who are living now in an abusive relationship, and can't seem to get away from it. Pray for those counselors and organizations that work with people in these situations. Pray for people you know who are looking for the "living water" in all the wrong places.

Chapter 24 A&B

Modern Woman: The Worldly Woman – Response: Remember Lot's Wife

TEXT: Genesis 19: 1-26

1. How are these two women alike?
2. How are they different?
3. What is the problem with becoming too content with worldly surroundings and possessions?
4. What was Lot's wife's dilemma?
5. How did God show His concern and care for Lot's wife?
6. How did she miss all the warning signs?
7. Read Matthew 6:24; Colossians 3:2; Luke 12: 15-21, 33-34 Discuss

PRAYER TOPIC:

Pray for people who are blinded and dazzled by the world's attractions and have set their affection on the things of this world. Pray especially for young people who are bombarded in many ways through technology today to "get this" - "have this" – "be this" etc. Ask God to help them see and learn about the things that really matter for eternity! Pray about what you might do to influence a young person you know who may be struggling with "the world".

Chapter 25: - Heaven's Bread

TEXTS: Exodus 16: 4-5, 21-35: Exodus 39:36, 40:22-23; I Kings 17: 7-16; Judges 7: 8-15; Matthew 4: 1-4; John 6: 1-13,25-29; Matthew 26: 17-30; John 21: 1-14; Luke 24: 13-35; I Corinthians 10: 14-17; Isaiah 55:2; Psalm 34:8

1. *What is manna – and why did God send it?*
2. *Talk about the showbread, and its significance.*
3. *Recount the story of Gideon and the barley loaf of bread. How did this encourage Gideon?*
4. *Why do you think bread is called "the staff of life"?*
5. *How is Jesus the "true bread of life come down from heaven"?*
6. *Is it possible that each time we come together for a meal and "break bread together" that it could be a sacrament? Discuss.*
7. *How does Jesus satisfy our hunger and thirst? See Matthew 5:6*
8. *What in particular touched you from this story?*

PRAYER TOPIC:

Pray for those who are filling the hungry places of their lives with the wrong "food." Pray that they will come to know the bread that satisfies. Pray for yourself, that your life may become Christ's broken bread for someone else!

248

Chapter 26: - The Wedding Garment

**TEXTS: Isaiah 61:10; Genesis 3:21;
Deuteronomy 8: 2-4, 29:5; I Samuel 17:12-51;
Matthew 22: 1-14; John 19: 23-24;
Isaiah 64:6; Revelation 7: 9-10**

1. According to Isaiah 61:10, how does God dress us?
2. Discuss the special clothes God made for Adam and Eve as recorded in Genesis 3:21.
3. Why didn't God just leave Adam and Eve in their fig leaves?
4. Discuss how God clothed the children of Israel as recorded in Deuteronomy 8: 2-4, and 29:5. Why is this important to know?
5. Why didn't David need to wear armor when he faced the giant?
6. What are the garments God provides for us? See Isaiah 11:5; Matthew 6:28-29; I Peter 3: 3-4; Colossians 3: 12-15. Discuss.
7. What does it mean to be clothed with His grace?
8. Read II Timothy 3: 1-5, and discuss how this fits into the story.

PRAYER TOPIC:

Pray for those people who are like "wolves in sheep's clothing" – who want to come to the banquet, but do not want to "put on" the garments Jesus provides. Pray for those who are going through the motions, but are lacking a relationship with the Master!

Chapter 27: - Tracing His Steps

TEXTS: Luke 2: 41-50 (MSG) Matthew 3: 17 (NKJV) John i: 34b (NKJV) Matthew 4: 1-22; John 2: 1-11; Luke 7: 36-50; Acts 1: 9-12

1. Why do you think Jesus stayed behind in the temple in Jerusalem when He was twelve years old?
2. See Luke 2: 41 – 52. What do you think Jesus meant by His response to Mary and Joseph when they found Him in the temple?
3. Can you relate to these reflections of Mary? Why or why not?
4. How do you think Mary felt when she saw and heard about Jesus' miracles?
5. How do you think she felt when she saw Him associating with sinners and the like?
6. Do you think Simeon's words found in Luke 2: 35 stayed in Mary's heart and mind? Why or why not?
7. Why do you think Simeon spoke those words?
8. How do you suppose Mary felt when she saw Jesus ascend in Heaven?

PRAYER TOPIC:

Pray for those who know about Jesus – who may even know and quote the Bible – who think He was a good man and teacher, but who cannot accept Him as God's Son, and therefore their Savior. Pray for those who are blinded by false teachings about Jesus – or blinded by other religions that are false.

Chapter 28: - *What is that in your Hand?*

TEXTS: *Joshua 6: 17-25; II Kings 4: 1-7;*
Matthew 26: 7-13; Acts 9: 36-42

1. What was in Rahab's hand?
2. How did she use it for God and others?
3. What was in the widow's hand?
4. How did God use it for His glory?
5. What was in Mary's hand?
6. How did God use it to comfort Jesus and bless others?
7. What did Dorcas have in her hand?
8. How did she use it to help others?
9. What miracle happened in each life?
10. Why is it important to give back to God the gifts and abilities He has given to us?
11. What might happen if we don't give God what is in our hands?

PRAYER TOPIC:

Pray for those who are wrestling with God, seeking His will for their lives – His plan, and His purpose. Pray that God will give them the courage and faith to give Him what He has given to them – in their hands. Pray that we will all realize that God can use whatever we have in our hands for His glory!

List of Reference Books

While the Monologues included in this book are original, I wish to acknowledge the fact that I have been helped, encouraged and blessed in my research and writing of each chapter by the following reference books, in addition to the Bible, various translations.

All the Women of the Bible Zondervan Publishing House – Herbert Lockyer

Christmas Hearts Promise Press – copyright 2000 – Tim Roehl

Commentary on the Whole Bible - Zondervan Publishing House – Jamieson, Fausset and Brown

Commentary on the Whole Bible – copyright 1961 – Zondervan Publishing House Matthew Henry

God Came Near copyright 1987 Multnomah Press – Max Lucado

CPSIA information can be obtained at www.ICGtesting.com
Printed in the USA
LVOW11s2056141015

458273LV00001B/1/P